Tough Marriage

BY PAUL A. MICKEY

Conflict and Resolution (with Robert L. Wilson)
What New Creation? (with Robert L. Wilson)
Pastoral Assertiveness (with Gary Gamble)
Essentials of Wesleyan Theology
Marriage in the Middle Years

Tough Marriage

How to Make a Difficult Relationship Work

Paul A. Mickey, B.D., Ph.D.,
with William Proctor

William Morrow and Company, Inc.
New York

Library of Congress Cataloging in Publication Data

Mickey, Paul A., 1937–
    Tough marriage.

    1. Marriage—Religious aspects—Christianity.
I. Proctor, William. II. Title.
BV835.M52   1986   248.8′4   85-21449
ISBN 0-688-05038-7

Printed in the United States of America

First Edition

1 2 3 4 5 6 7 8 9 10

BOOK DESIGN BY RICHARD ORIOLO

TO JANE BECKER MICKEY
AND PAM PROCTOR

ACKNOWLEDGMENTS

We are extremely grateful to Esther Wrightsel and Laura Freed for their editorial and writing assistance in producing this manuscript.

CONTENTS

Tough Marriage

INTRODUCTION

What Is a Tough Marriage?

These days, only a special kind of lean-and-mean relationship can weather the storms of death, fire, flood—and even the threat of divorce. You can pull these muscular marriages, push them, stretch them to the limit, and they'll still take a little more punishment. In fact, they'll emerge stronger than ever before.

I'm talking about twosomes that can only be described as tough. This is the fifty- or sixty-year kind that calls for celebrations, causes stirring speeches, inspires other couples, and provides total satisfaction, guaranteed for a lifetime.

The beautiful thing about such a long-term love relationship is this: It's available to everybody. The sad thing is that few people seem to be able to get to first base in achieving the goal. These are rough times for husband-wife ties. Only special kinds of marriages have any chance of survival over the long haul. Only the most resilient can bounce back after really bad times. Why the failure? The main problem is that we've lost sight of the basic universal principles that must underlie a tough, durable marriage. So what I want to do in the following pages is to reintroduce you to the foundations of truly authentic husband-wife love and suggest some ways you can use these precepts to build up your own relationship.

As you may know, there once was a time when marriage was considered a permanent affair. Newlyweds, along with their family and friends, assumed that in tying the knot, they were establishing an unbreakable bond. The "till-death-do-us-part" vow was taken seriously. The matrimonial relationship was the cornerstone of a stable family and, even more, a stable society.

·But today, the situation has changed drastically. Marriage as an institution is under fire. Some fear it's already suffered fatal wounds. I even know people who avoid congratulating engaged couples because of the rocky roads that likely lie ahead, ready to wreck the husband-wife tie. After all, we live in an age when about half of all marriages break up. Temporariness, rather than permanence, is becoming the norm for the conjugal state. In short, some pundits assume that truly stable, lifetime relationships are becoming as obsolete as the dinosaur.

As a result of the breakup of so many marriages and the bad track record of others, a kind of spiritual pall has settled over this venerable institution. Growing numbers of people seem willing to settle for less than the best. They believe insuperable problems are inevitable, and so when even minor problems pop up, they may be more inclined to give up and not "tough it out."

But is this pessimism really justified? Is there really no hope? Is it indeed virtually impossible to count on an old-fashioned lifetime husband-wife relationship?

My answer to each of these questions is a resounding "No! No! No!" In brief, this is why:

In every historic era, a high premium has been placed on the marriage relationship. The ancient Hebrews thought the marital tie was so important that adultery was punishable by death. Adultery was also a crime in early Rome, even though—as was also the case under Jewish law—it was considered an offense only when the *woman* was married to another person.

In 1650, the second year of the Commonwealth government of England, adultery was declared a capital crime. The death penalty was removed after the Restoration, but even today adultery remains a crime under many modern statutes. In many jurisdictions, both the man and woman are considered guilty if either is married to another party.

So this message comes across loud and clear in various legal traditions: Violations of the marriage contract won't be tolerated. Okay, you may say. But why have stable marriages always been so important to the survival of a civilization?

First of all, a stable, peaceful society must be based, at least in part, on solid, faithful family life. If marriages are constantly crumbling, children will lose their primary source of moral guidance. Crime and emotional problems begin to run rampant. Instability flourishes. Anarchy flows from the family roots, upward and downward.

Secondly, when marriages break up on a regular basis, the family as a stable economic unit also disintegrates. Once again, society as a whole begins to suffer. The foundations for accumulating capital and building successful farms and businesses fall by the wayside. Economic chaos ensues.

Finally, there seems to be something in the basic nature of things that calls for stable family life. Now I know this may sound a little mystical, but think about it for a moment: The earliest moral codes required some recognition of long-term marriage stability. Moreover, up until only about the last couple of decades, those codes were the main standards that most of us followed. Certainly, there were people who violated them or who rejected them outright as invalid. But the majority of people at least regarded a stable lifetime marital relationship as a good thing, something worth trying to achieve.

Things have changed considerably in the last couple of

decades. More of us are uncertain that the ancient, time-tested standards are valid. Growing numbers are sure they aren't valid. But our attraction to the amoral fashions of the moment can't change reality.

We can't, just by saying gravity doesn't exist, get rid of it and begin to float at will through the air. We can't pretend that a car hurtling directly toward us is not going to hit us. By the same token, we can't say marriage doesn't matter and expect to escape unscathed.

There are certain scientific and physical principles of life that we take for granted and respect. If we try to ignore any of them—say, the law of gravity—we do so at our peril. In the same way, there are rules for sexual relationships. I can't explain exactly why they are there any more than I can explain some of the bedrock truths of chemistry or physics. But I do have a good idea about what those principles are—and what the consequences are of violating them.

In short, I believe that the experience of mankind over the centuries has demonstrated that there is a right way to run a marriage and also a wrong way. Furthermore, the guidelines for the right way can be distilled into what I call the twelve commandments for a tough marriage.

You've probably heard of many of these commandments before. But hearing of them is one thing; applying them is quite another. In my marital counseling and research, I've discovered that most people have real trouble making use of these principles these days. So it's my intent in this book to explain these commandments in a new light by showing you how you can employ them in practical ways in your own marriage.

To sum up, the twelve commandments we'll be exploring can be stated this way:

1. Put your mate on a pedestal.
2. Kiss Mom and Dad goodbye.
3. Speak the truth in love.
4. Break bread together.

5. Strengthen your spouse's character.
6. Make a commitment to a community of faith.
7. Get rid of the lust in your life.
8. Swing into a slow-motion style.
9. Prepare for the pits instead of the peaks.
10. Learn to master new marital tricks.
11. Fight for some solitude.
12. Learn to let go.

Now, I should mention right at the outset a couple of basic principles that underlie these commandments. First of all, I'm hard-nosed about the need to follow them. Not only do I think they're all important, but I'm also convinced that if you break one of them, you break them all. It's not that you have to be a perfect person to have a perfect marriage. But you do have to be making solid progress in *all* twelve of these areas if you hope to be a successful, satisfied husband or wife.

Secondly, even though I may speak individually of the husband and the wife, I think it's essential to recognize that when a man and woman get married, they really do become one. The book of Genesis says, "a man leaves his father and mother and cleaves to his wife, and they become one flesh." And Jesus later affirms this principle when he says of a married couple, "the two become one." I take those words at their face value. I've become convinced in my experience with a variety of couples that the only way a marriage will really work is for the man and woman to merge, almost in a mystical sense.

I realize, of course, that such a statement may not sit too well at first with those who are concerned about maintaining the rights and autonomy of the individual. But quite frankly, if you want your marriage to work, you have to quit focusing on your rights and concentrate instead on the unity of the relationship.

To put this idea in more concrete, practical terms, it's necessary to understand that:

- when your wife hurts, so do you.
- when your husband has certain needs, those needs are yours as well.
- when you make a good impression on others, so does your spouse.
- when you grow emotionally or spiritually, your mate grows as well.

Whether you like it or not, the two of you really do become a single entity in many respects after marriage. You can either acknowledge this fact and learn to benefit from it and even celebrate it, or you can deny this radical oneness, begin to live separate lives, and watch your marriage deteriorate.

So "obeying" all the twelve commandments and affirming a revolutionary kind of unity in your marriage are two underlying, universal principles that undergird a successful marriage. But I find that many people wonder, before they launch a revolutionary marriage program, "How can I tell how healthy my marriage is right now?" And after they've started incorporating the twelve commandments into their relationship, they ask, "How can I check to see how I'm progressing in toughening up my matrimonial ties?"

As an ongoing test of the viability of your marriage, you may find it helpful to ask yourself these key questions:

Tough Marriage Test #1: Is my first response to stand firm or to run when things get rough?
To put it bluntly, if you hold out the possibility of walking out on your mate or getting a divorce if things don't work out, you're not sufficiently committed. You're not tough enough.

The word *commitment* is tossed around too lightly these days, and that's one of the reasons I frequently avoid it. I like *obligation* better because it suggests something much more serious and onerous. That's what we need a strong dose of—a heavyweight stand-and-fight attitude, an absolutely binding sense of responsibility. If you think it's possible your marriage will fail, then it definitely will fail. No doubt about it. There are too many disruptive pressures on marriages these days to permit any tentative commitments to survive.

Quite frankly, many of us haven't really grown up. We insist on holding on to our private freedoms so that we can do pretty much what we want to do in the marriage. We don't want to tie up our time or money in doing for others. We just don't care enough for others to make the effort. And this selfishness spills over into family life.

Grown children often have little or no sense of responsibility for their aging parents and other family members. Mother Teresa of Calcutta has told various Western audiences that they should stop dreaming about trying to help the poorest of the poor on the streets of India and look instead to the poor in their midst—including their own neglected spouses or their elderly mothers or fathers who have been filed away in nursing homes.

By the same token, many parents seem to feel little obligation to spend time with their young kids. It's hard to get many people interested in family vacations anymore, mainly because each person wants to focus on recreation that will satisfy his or her personal needs. There's slight commitment to any relationship as a whole.

I'm well aware of the wrenching forces that put great strains on commitment in my own family today. Some of the most positive memories of my childhood in Ohio center around our family's summer camping trips. My parents had made a commitment that we would go to a different part of the country each year, and so we traveled to Washington, D.C., Chicago, New York, and other places. We didn't go first-class. In fact, we had an old canvas tent we used whenever we could. But we did do things together.

More recently, though, my own wife and I have found it's harder to generate interest in family vacations. For one thing, we have more money than my folks did and more available transportation, so we can each go off and do pretty much what we like by ourselves, without relying on family support systems. Also, everybody in our family—and in many other families we know—gets so busy with individual activities, it's hard for everyone to break free at the same time and schedule any extended periods of joint recreation.

Finally, big family vacations are often not regarded as the "in" thing nowadays. Kids want to be more independent, and sometimes even spouses feel they need separate vacations to get away from one another. Whatever the reasons, there are pressures that make it harder to do things together as a family.

Unfortunately, if we allow ourselves to go too far in this direction, husbands and wives become individuals again. The unity of the relationship is destroyed. And when really bad times come along, the marital fiber isn't strong enough to hold up.

In one relationship I've observed, the marriage was going along fairly smoothly. The pitched battles between husband and wife were few and far between. But one of the reasons was that the two were apart quite often. Both spouses worked and were deeply involved in different community activities, and so they saw each other only for limited periods. As a result, there was little opportunity for fights to develop. Moreover, they were both in good health and there was plenty of money. The children were relatively well mannered and were making good grades. Everything seemed to be going along swimmingly—until the wife was struck down with cancer.

So here we are presented with a disturbing but highly effective way to test the toughness of a marriage: That is, how well does it do in the face of a tragic loss of health?

In this case, the couple didn't fare too well. Their sex life disappeared while the wife was bedridden. The kids, feeling the pressure and fearing the possible loss of a parent, became preoccupied with the home crisis—and their performance and attitude at school suffered. This meant more discussions, counseling, and arguments about the kids' problems. The "in-sickness-and-health" part of the marriage vow tested the husband severely, since he had to care for the kids, play nurse to his wife, and give up the satisfactions of an active sex life.

Unfortunately, he was tested and found wanting. First came tremendous fatigue and frustration. Then, self-pity took over. Finally, he found excuses to start cheating on his wife. She eventually recovered, but the marriage didn't. The challenges of the illness were too tough for the marriage, and divorce was the result. The sense of obligation and deep commitment to make it work, come hell or high water, simply wasn't there.

In another cancer crisis, a second couple didn't have a particularly deep philosophy of life. They just had an old-fashioned attitude, expressed this way by the husband: "Hey, we made a permanent commitment back when we got married, and now we're just going to grit our teeth and stick it out! If I were sick, she'd take care of me—thank God. And so you can bet I'm going to take care of her now, when she's fighting the big C."

And he did.

Tough Marriage Test #2: Do I think in terms of "we" rather than "I"?

Individualism is held up as a great virtue in our society. But the same "I" orientation that can build great businesses or produce great works of art will inevitably sound the death knell of a marriage.

Too often, we only enter into a marriage for what we can get out of it. It's an optional arrangement, a kind of disposable consumer item that we can throw away at will. What are the wrong reasons for getting into a marriage? Here are some of the main ones I've run into:

- I want social status.
- I want to be married, like everyone else.
- At my age, I should be married.
- I can't stand any more pressure from my parents.
- I'm tired of the pressure to get married from the person I'm living with.
- I want the added economic convenience.

- I want to consummate my current romantic attachment, like they do in the romance novels.
- I'm an insecure person, and I need more protection.
- I want companionship.
- I want somebody sleeping beside me every night.
- I need to fulfill a number of emotional needs.
- I want somebody to replace Mommy or Daddy.

All these reasons concentrate on "I," and if they continue to be of primary importance *after* the marriage, you've got real trouble on your hands. As we've already seen, marriage is essentially a unified relationship, in which two people must in a very real sense become one. But if you focus on "I" instead of on "we," that unity will immediately get into trouble. You see, it's entirely too natural and easy to begin a relationship thinking only of what you can get out of it. Then you start automatically pursuing *your* interests at every turn instead of the *joint* interests of you and your mate.

For example, I know one married man who recently bought a big touring motorcycle that cost close to five thousand dollars. He got it because he gets a real charge out of being on the open road; moreover, just having it sitting in his garage provides him with a sense of pride.

But there's a problem with this motorcycle. He and his wife have an eighteen-month-old child and they never use baby-sitters, so she is tied down to the home for much of the week. The only possible days they could spend together as a family are Saturday and Sunday, but the husband feels those are ideal days to hit the road on his touring machine. So he heads for motorcycle races or the open road, for good times with his cycling buddies. His wife and child are left at home alone regularly and forced to fend for themselves and bear the weight of his weekend rejection.

It became clear to me after several counseling sessions that this guy's marriage was definitely on a down elevator. By spending so much time and money doing only what he wanted to do—rather than what he should have been doing as a husband and a father—he was putting a great strain on his marriage. He followed his own personal agenda. He wouldn't accept a joint agenda, a joint commitment to his wife and daughter.

It's not surprising that his marriage began to break down. In our sessions together, his conversation was punctuated by such phrases as "my needs" and "my personal rights." So we first concentrated on getting him to see his relationship with his wife in terms of "we" rather than "I."

I've become convinced that when I hear a person talk about "my needs," those are code words for immaturity, self-ishness, and low self-esteem. Of course I'm not saying you shouldn't say, right up front to your spouse, "What I want out of this relationship is thus-and-so and I think you might do such-and-such to help me achieve these goals." But in the same breath, it's important to ask, "What do you want out of our relationship?" Another important question is: "What do you want from *me* in the relationship?"

Also, your own feelings and desires have to be presented as suggestions and requests, not nonnegotiable demands. In some ways, a marriage is like a labor-management contract dispute. Once one spouse states a concern or desire, negotiation of some sort should always follow. In this way, the couple, together, can find what's best for their total relationship and not just for one member of the team.

Another couple that came to me for help had a similar problem with this "I" psychology. The man owned a small airplane and kept referring to it as "my baby." He also drove a turbo Audi with all the accouterments and talked about that machine the same way—as "my baby." Ironically, his wife wanted to have a child and she constantly referred to her dream as "my baby."

I pointed out to them that it would be appropriate to talk about "our airplane," "our Audi," and "our baby." They agreed immediately, and the entire tone of the discussion changed—from self-centered concerns to a focus on the couple's joint needs.

It continues to amaze me what a power there is in pointing out the basic unity of the marriage relationship. Most people who really want to have a better, stronger marriage seem to understand instinctively that they are *one* in their relationship and not two. Unfortunately, the emphasis of the popular media on self-fulfillment has obscured the power of this principle of unity. It's time to recapture this truth if we hope to make our marriages work.

Tough Marriage Test #3:   Is your marriage strong enough to make it when you have to move to new surroundings?
In our mobile society, most couples can expect to move from one part of the country to another a number of times. Unfortunately, those moves put some of the greatest stresses possible on individuals and marriage relationships.

Several factors seem responsible. Worries multiply about the details of life, such as finding a new home, shifting furniture around, setting up new bank accounts, and making contacts with local shops. New friends must be made. New churches and community support groups have to be found. In short, many of a couple's important roots and spiritual support systems are lost, and this places a great premium on the stability of the marriage relationship itself.

If your marriage is tough, a move may still be hard—but it certainly won't be impossible. On the other hand, if your marriage is weak, the strains may be too much for the relationship to bear.

Tough Marriage Test #4: Can you handle "intruders" in your home?
I'm not talking about burglars or break-in artists. Rather, the intruder could be any disruptive surprise: It may be an unwelcome visiting friend or relative; an unexpected doctor bill; a flood in the basement that requires some time and money

to correct; or a TV sporting event or mini-series. It doesn't matter how trivial the intruder may seem to an outsider. The important thing is how irritating it may be to you or your spouse.

For example, I know one husband who was far less open to entertaining visitors—especially those who might spend the night—than was his wife. The wife, sometimes without thinking twice, would invite people to stay over and sometimes they accepted, to the husband's great annoyance.

The cumulative effect of these and other misunderstandings and the arguments that resulted from them began to wear on the marriage, and so the pair came to me for help. It took several sessions to identify all the "little" problems that had begun to loom so large, such as their disagreement about how to handle visitors. But when the couple finally got all their cards on the table, they were in a better position to deal with minor crises, and the result was a stronger, more mature relationship.

Such intrusions can cause a sense that your home has been violated. You may feel you're being forced to the end of your rope by circumstances beyond your control. A tough marriage will weather these intrusions. But a weak relationship can be further damaged in the face of such challenges.

Tough Marriage Test #5: Do you regard divorce as an option?
If you do—if you sometimes think at the back of your mind, Well, if things get too bad, we can always split and I can start over again—then you're treading on dangerous territory. I've discovered that even if a spouse jokes about getting a divorce, such an attitude can be the first step toward seriously considering a separation.

A major problem with joking about divorce or, worse, holding it out as a viable option, is that this kind of thinking trivializes your marriage. It makes your relationship something much less serious than it is designed to be. A really resilient marriage relation—one that's tough enough to last through thick and thin—involves assumptions on the part of both spouses that it's a "forever proposition."

To put this another way, a marriage must be *the* thing you want in life, not one of the things. When the conjugal bond becomes just one of the items you desire—almost the same way you might want a four-speaker stereo for the car—you greatly reduce the chances of the marriage working. So any consideration of divorce is a first step toward disaster. Even fantasizing about divorce is an act of aggression against both yourself, and your spouse, for divorce is death of an eternal relationship.

In the most practical terms, divorce is like a forest fire that ravages an entire countryside. It burns down what's in front of it and leaves behind an ugliness and vulnerability, a sense in all concerned of being violated. In a divorce, it doesn't matter whether you are the one who started the fire or whether you just got caught in the middle of it. Whenever a marriage is seared to its roots, no one emerges uninjured.

At one time or another, every marriage runs into difficulties. The road to success will never be completely smooth and easy. Even if you go through a honeymoon period of several years, there will always be trials and tribulations that you must confront down the road. But if you make up your mind to develop a tough marriage, you'll find that you can make your relationship work during any challenging period.

In the following pages, the twelve commandments of a tough marriage have been designed to help you make it through the valleys and over the mountains that are bound to block your way toward that ultimate goal of a supremely rewarding relationship. But I want to emphasize once again: It won't do to pick and choose the commandments you want to follow and ignore those that seem distasteful or less important. When God gave the original Ten Commandments and the other laws to Moses and ancient Israel, He said that violating one was tantamount to breaking them all. And so it is with these commandments for a tough marriage.

Certainly, I'm not setting my twelve commandments on a par with God's ten in the book of Exodus. Yet like the original ten, the principles contained in these twelve imperatives can be found in Holy Scripture, as well as in the most successful contemporary marriages. They have the imprimatur of divine approval. They have their roots in the words of the priests and the prophets, in the universal laws of personal relationships. They are nonnegotiable basics for a successful marriage relationship.

So now, with this background and basic approach in mind, let's move on to the first of matrimonial maxims—the command to put your mate on a pedestal.

THE FIRST COMMANDMENT

Put Your Mate on a Pedestal

For the past few years, the book market has been flooded by "self-help" guides offering cure-alls to take care of everything from credit ratings to waistlines. The news media have further encouraged self-fulfillment with a startling variety of practical advice columns. In addition, there is the current crop of videotapes and cassette recordings and a cornucopia of special classes to bolster our efforts toward self-gratification.

The message is "self, self, self." In some ways, I suppose that's not such a bad thing because many of us have tended to downgrade our basic worth as individuals. Also, too often we've let ourselves go—intellectually, physically, and spiritually. So a little nudging toward self-improvement may sometimes be a healthy influence. We all can use an extra dose of self-esteem.

But there are also some major problems with these increasingly self-centered programs. You see, the more we focus on ourselves, the less aware we become of others—and the less attention we pay to their needs. Such a preoccupation with personal concerns can have a negative effect on our sense of priorities. And for a marriage relationship, distorted priorities may prove fatal in no time at all.

My first commandment for a successful marriage—that you should put your mate on a pedestal—flies right in the face of many values that have emerged in our excessively self-centered society. This rule is rather radical and will probably even strike some people as stupid, at least at first.

To put it bluntly, I believe that each partner must learn to put the best interests of his or her spouse above his or her own. In other words, it's necessary to abandon the old "look-out-for-number-one" syndrome; and it's essential to give up those narcissistic attitudes that say, I only have to do what makes me feel good.

But what, you may ask, does such a pedestal principle of husband-wife relationships do to our concept of equal rights of men and women? My answer: It gives them a new life and broader impact! Remember, I didn't say that only women should put men on a pedestal *or* that only men should put women up there. No; this pedestal commandment applies to *both* men and women—equally.

But still, something seems a little off, doesn't it? After all, in our self-help society, we're used to wrestling with our own problems and letting the other person, even the spouse, take care of his or her own. And that's just the problem! Most of us are constantly trying to build ourselves up and struggling to fulfill our own potential, whatever that is. At the same time, we fail to realize that when we get married, we're no longer little islands unto ourselves. We're not just two people who happen to be married; we're now two in one. In fact, we are two who have *become* one. The happiness, satisfaction, and fulfillment of the wife depends on that of the husband, and vice versa.

But why, you may ask, put the other mate on a pedestal? Isn't that going a little far?

To answer such objections, it's necessary to understand ex-

actly what a pedestal is. According to most common defini-
tions, it's something that serves as a support or foundation. In
fact, the pedestal that you are building for your spouse and
that he is building for you is the very foundation for your entire marriage. It's the *mutual* basis for a fulfilling relationship.
We've already established that a man and woman become
one in marriage. And when two become one, there is no
longer room solely for individual rights. In a way, you might
even say there are no longer any individual rights at all in the
relationship. Instead, the corporate rights of the couple take
precedence over all else as a genuine joint identity emerges
from the matrimonial alliance.

One of the best ways of achieving this oneness is for each
to raise the concerns and needs of the other above his own. In
other words, one spouse first accords his mate a lofty position
of honor and respect; the mate then responds in kind. The
result is that both partners begin to benefit significantly, as
each continues to lift up the other.

Traditionally, men and women have gravitated toward different sets of duties and responsibilities in their domestic
lives. Often, it hasn't made much difference what the law or
formal social policies have said the position of men and
women should be—at least, not on the grassroots level of the
marriage. The key thing has been how a given couple works
things out in practice.

In the mid-nineteenth century in the United States, when
the concept of women's rights was still in its infancy, the
practicalities of married life dictated a kind of de facto equality. James D. Burn, an Englishman who published *Three
Years among the Working Classes in the United States during the War* in 1965, said that the roles and rights of the sexes
had in effect been "reversed" in many cases in America.

Often, he noted, the husband did "a considerable part of
the slip-slop work," or household tasks that were normally associated with the duties of the wife. This included stoking up
a fire in the morning, emptying the slop buckets, cooking his

own breakfast, making a lunch for himself, and then heading off to work—while his wife was still sound asleep!

"Even among the trading classes who have private dwellings, it is quite common to see the men bringing parcels from the market, the grocer's, fishmonger's, or butcher's, for the next day's meal," Burn said.

In other cultures, the duties and powers actually exercised by the husband may be entirely different from those of the wife. But they aren't necessarily accorded a higher or more important status. In fact, in many stable, "advanced" societies, each mate in the relationship seems to achieve a generally equal status of special respect in his or her particular realm.

For example, in early Greek times, beginning during the Homeric age of perhaps the tenth century B.C., the wife held a position equal to that of her husband, according to the *Dictionary of Classical Antiquities*. They each held sway in different spheres, and she commanded the same respect in hers as he did in his. The clear implication is that they had to recognize and support each other in achieving their respective identities and fulfilling their distinct sets of responsibilities. In short, each had to put the other on the proper pedestal.

The same tendency is apparent in New Testament times. As much as the apostle Paul is sometimes unfairly maligned for his supposed "anti-female" attitudes, he actually advocated that the husband should subordinate his interests to his wife's.

First of all, he made it clear that in the Christian community "there is neither male nor female; for you are all one in Christ Jesus" (Galatians 3:28). It's hard to conceive of a more definitive statement of equality. Then he went further. He commanded, "Husbands, love your wives, as Christ loved the church and gave himself up for her . . ." (Ephesians 5:25). In other words, the man's role in a marriage was to be characterized primarily by service and sacrifice. He was to put his wife's interests above his own.

Of course, Paul didn't put the burden on just the husband.
And this is where some of the distortions and misunderstandings about Paul's teachings come in. He certainly did say,
". . . let wives be subject in everything to their husbands."
But that was only fair, since the husband, for his part, was expected to lift his wife up to lofty heights.

Then, it seems to me that he more or less wrapped everything up in his letter to the Ephesians when he urged husbands *and* wives to *serve one another*. That is, he advocated
the principle that each should put the other on a pedestal
(Ephesians 5:21).

As I've counseled various couples, I've found that these
historical precedents and principles are valid for today as well.
But the pedestal plan, which has such ancient and deep roots,
clearly requires certain preconditions for those who expect it
to enhance their marriage.

First of all, there has to be a two-way commitment.

Secondly, putting your mate on a pedestal can't involve a
subtle form of manipulation to achieve your own goals. It has
to be a sincere gesture of love.

A third precondition is that one of the partners must take
the first step. In the beginning, it may seem a little scary to
start putting someone else's interests above your own, even
when that person happens to be your husband or wife.

Finally, for a time—and maybe even indefinitely—one
spouse may have to be the sole party who is living by the ped-
estal-building rules. In other words, when you begin to build
your mate up and start putting his interests above your own,
he might not respond in the way you expect. In fact, he may
not respond at all. Fortunately, though, when one spouse
takes the initiative, the other usually will respond as well. It
may take a week, a month, even a year. But believe me—if
you begin to build a solid pedestal for your mate, the chances
are he will eventually start building one for you.

But what exactly makes up the pedestal?

To construct a pedestal for your spouse that is going to

support a truly tough, resilient marriage, you need ten building blocks. But take care. If you fail to select these foundation stones wisely and don't put them in place properly, you may find that the many pressures of life will cause the entire structure to crumble. In that case, your mate may come tumbling down squarely on top of you, and you could lose your entire marriage and family in the ensuing catastrophe.

Now, let's take a look at those ten building blocks that have the power to support the pedestal you can build for your mate.

Building Block #1:   *Make sacrifices.*
Sacrifice is an old-fashioned notion in the minds of many, yet it's one that has stood the test of time and deserves first place in the list of the building blocks that make up your mate's pedestal.

We get our first introduction to sacrifice in marriage the day after the wedding. Every husband and wife has to give something up. As single people, we develop certain rituals for waking up, eating, and entertaining ourselves. We live in our own little spheres, making independent decisions about how to spend our time, energy, and money. Then, in a matter of a few short hours, we're no longer one; we're two in one. Now everything is different.

Knowing what to give up—and *when* to let it go—is one of the most difficult lessons of any marriage. For example, before marriage, many people spend at least one night a week in some type of social activity. It may be anything from bowling to bar hopping, but the distinctive thing about this pursuit is that it's *yours.* You've chosen it because for some reason it gives you great satisfaction and it's become an ingrained part of your life. But when you get married, you can no longer assume that your former lifestyle, including this number-one, absolutely favorite activity of yours, is going to give the same satisfaction to your new spouse.

One of the couples I've counseled had just such a problem

of adjustment. The young man was a very fine volleyball player who took much pleasure in playing the sport as often as possible. The usual time for his workout was in the evening, and he scheduled several games each week.

His new wife, however, resented his spending so much time playing volleyball. In fact, he was away so many evenings that his absences began to affect their relationship. "Is this what I got married for—to sit home alone every day after work?" she protested. "I did better than that when I was single!"

To avoid endangering the very foundation of their marriage, the man finally began to understand that he had to change his ways. Obviously, he had to cut down on playing so much volleyball. It was an activity that had provided him with a great deal of male companionship and had become very much a part of his personal identity. But now his marriage had to take precedence.

In this case, by the way, the husband didn't give up his sport altogether. But he did stop going to the gymnasium every day after work, as he had done when he was single. His wife just needed to know that she was more important to him than volleyball. And he needed to understand that his relationship to her was more important than a ball and net. The change in the amount of time he spent on volleyball was a necessary sacrifice to shore up the foundations of the relationship. It was a positive gesture that strengthened his wife's pedestal and put the marriage back on a solid footing.

Building Block #2: Encourage feelings of security in your mate.

It's important for each spouse to feel secure about the other, because uncertainty or anxiety can wreck havoc on the stability of a marriage relationship.

Some people like to suggest that keeping the other spouse off balance injects a little "mystery" and hence romance into a relationship. The "lady-killer" or "femme fatale" before marriage may argue *after* the wedding that things will stay more interesting if the other party thinks he or she is still highly desirable to other people. Or the independent adventurer of either sex may believe an attitude that evokes an "I-wonder-what-he's-doing-now" response will add some needed zip and excitement.

But don't you believe it! These are just thinly veiled rationalizations for maintaining a degree of independence that simply doesn't mesh with strong marital bonds. If your spouse can't count on you implicitly and isn't fairly sure about your loyalties, you've got problems in your future, my friend!

Fortunately, if a lack of a sense of security about you or the relationship happens to be your mate's main problem, there are some simple but highly effective corrective measures you can take. The best procedure is to: 1) identify the precise source of the insecurity; 2) talk about it so that you become thoroughly sensitive to your spouse's feelings and needs; and 3) take concrete steps to eliminate the problem.

During one marriage-enrichment retreat, a husband I know mentioned that he was concerned when his wife arrived home from work later than normal. She is a nurse who works the "graveyard," or late-night, shift at a health-care facility. In this case, he wasn't worried that she might be out with another man. What bothered him was that she might be mugged or otherwise molested when she commuted back and forth on deserted streets in the dead of night.

So we sat down, did the simple three-step analysis of the problem, and came up with this solution: The wife now phones home immediately when she walks into the hospital to begin work. Also, at the end of work she calls if her shift runs late, if she plans to stop for gasoline, or if there's some other delay.

By this simple procedure, she has shown that she is aware of her husband's insecurity, she's sensitive to his feelings, and she's ready to act to ease the problem. She goes out of her way to elevate his concerns and interests above what might come more naturally to her. As a result, their marriage is more solid.

Building Block #3: *Be open in expressing love to your spouse.*

Many people, women as well as men, find it difficult to take the initiative in showing affection for a mate. It's ironic, isn't it, that we resist displays of love when marriage is supposed to be based on a special deep tie between a man and a woman? Yet there's sometimes a reluctance to bare our feelings to the one we've chosen to share our most intimate moments.

Telling or showing our spouse how much we care puts him or her well above us, even if for a brief moment. Symbolically, in these situations we have to fall to our knees before the other person, and that makes us more vulnerable.

When you say, "I'm so lucky to be married to you," you let your defenses down. There's an outside chance that you may even get hurt. What if your mate says, "If you feel so lucky, why don't you show it more often?" That's a put-down that probably won't happen. But there's always the fear that it may occur. And it's these remote fears that make us build walls to protect ourselves and keep our love bottled up inside.

Unfortunately, this all too common attitude tends to topple our mate from the pedestal, and the marriage as a whole suffers. You have to show love if you hope to receive it. Expressions of love can range from preparing a favorite dish to remembering a special day to an intimate bit of romance. Sometimes, the simplest overtures of affection are the most powerful. When feelings of distance and coldness have been allowed to creep in, just a pat or a hug can completely close the gap between you and your spouse.

On the other side of the coin, it's often as difficult to accept ourselves as love objects as it is to show love. It may be hard for you to believe that someone can love you with great depth and affection. But when your spouse takes the initiative toward you, just accept the fact that you are being offered a deserved bit of honor and esteem, that you're loved and lovable. If you assume you're worthy of affection, care, and esteem, you'll become more worthy and you'll enjoy and accept love more easily.

Even more important; when your mate makes the first move, she may well feel hurt if you reject or fail to notice her gesture. So you have to let yourself be important to your mate. Otherwise, you'll make it impossible for her to put *you* on a pedestal! And remember: In the most effective marriage, each spouse must be elevated by the other.

Building Block #4: Reduce unnecessary pressures on your spouse.

We live in a pressure-cooker society, with incredible demands placed on both men and women, who are supposed to be perfect parents, high-performance workers, and superior spouses. The more money you have and the better educated you are, the more the demands seem to accelerate. But if you don't take steps to help depressurize the demands on your mate, you could both end up facing some serious difficulties.

The primary rule here is *caution* in expecting too much of your mate. No amount of herculean effort or enterprising encouragement will make either one of you Superman or Wonder Woman.

I know a young couple who almost wrecked their marriage by trying to become picture-perfect partners. The young man was in graduate school at the time, and his wife was on the public relations staff of a large corporation. Both were working hard to make ends meet and to achieve their common goal of the good life. But the big problem came from their incompatible schedules. The young man didn't have classes until nine or ten o'clock in the morning, so he stayed up nights doing research. He was naturally a "night person" anyhow, and he seemed to do his best work in the wee hours of the morning.

His wife, on the other hand, had to be at work early: She liked to be at her desk by 8:00 A.M. She tended to be a "morning person," and also, she needed a lot of sleep to function best. Nine hours a night was her preference. That meant she had to get up before 6:00 A.M., and so she regularly tried to get to bed quite early.

The main conflict for the couple came in those mid-evening hours, when she was winding down and he was winding up. He liked to enjoy an elegant, leisurely dinner, read the paper, chat for a while, and then make love before hitting the books. But by then, his wife was exhausted from a long day at work and from doing her daily household tasks. When nine o'clock came around, she was ready for a good night's sleep.

Neither person was happy with this living arrangement, and both had become thoroughly frustrated with the pressures they were experiencing. As we talked about the problem, it became evident that neither really knew what the other wanted. The wife was wearing herself out preparing a magnificent three-course meal, which she assumed he expected. The husband, in turn, had begun to make fewer demands on her sexually because it seemed to him that she just wasn't the type who got "turned on."

So we began to explore ways to reduce the pressures in their marriage. The husband readily agreed that a light meal, which would take just a few minutes to prepare, would be just as acceptable as a heavy one. He liked gourmet meals, but not as much as he liked a calm, responsive, energetic wife. Also, he postponed his newspapers, and they did their casual chatting in the bedroom.

In effect, by eliminating pressures that had inadvertently begun to plague his wife, he helped lift her up to a new level of relaxation and peace. One thing led to another, and they soon found that their sex life was back on track again. Also, there was still time for the wife to get plenty of sleep before her early morning wake-up.

Once this couple talked and planned ways to depressurize their marriage, they were able to work out their differences more realistically. They abandoned any pretensions to perfection and adjusted their expectations of one another.

Building Block #5:   Don't feel you have to pay for the pedestal!
Sometimes one spouse or the other assumes that expensive presents or vacations are the best way to raise a mate to a worthy position. This is a total distortion of the pedestal principle!

Financial problems are always listed, along with sex, as a top cause of marital discord. No matter how long you've been married, money can be a sensitive topic that can rip a relationship apart. And I can't think of a better way to get into big trouble than to think you can put your wife on a pedestal by buying her a diamond bracelet or a fur coat; or to believe that you can elevate your husband to the aeries by dipping into the family finances to purchase him an expensive watch or other extravagances.

Of course, if you have plenty of discretionary income, you may be able to afford such luxuries. But most of us don't possess that kind of cash. And even if you do, it's easy to get fooled into thinking you can buy the pedestal rather than build it.

Quite often, the problem begins when young couples become sloppy with their household accounts. Most young marrieds who are just starting out must operate under some financial restrictions. They may even discuss the need for a budget and set one up. But then a temptation to purchase something unusual comes along, and the budget goes down the drain.

For example, one young fellow got rather bored with his everyday routine, and he suggested to his wife that they splurge a little with a Caribbean vacation. She was somewhat concerned because she knew they didn't have any extra money at the moment. But not wanting to make her husband unhappy, she agreed, and off they went.

Unfortunately, her reservations about the extraordinary expense proved justified. When the bills for the vacation started coming in, they found they didn't have the cash to cover them. So they had to borrow from their credit line at the bank, and the burden of those monthly payments with interest far outweighed the pleasure of their island trip.

A more realistic suggestion for the wife to have made would have been, "Why don't we spend a week at this nearby beach or that local mountain resort?" They could have enjoyed a pleasant, short trip, perhaps just a weekend away by themselves, which would probably have accomplished as much for the husband as the more expensive junket to the Caribbean. And just as important, she would have avoided agreeing to use the family money unwisely to "pay for a pedestal" for her husband.

So even as you try to shore up the position of your spouse, be realistic about your financial limitations and stay within the constraints of your budget. A solid financial base will go a long way toward holding your pedestals in place.

Building Block #6: Help your spouse fight fear.
All of us harbor a special set of fears. We may be afraid of having children, of moving to a new community, or even of flying in an airplane. If the things that scare your mate affect your marriage in any way, then it's essential to help him confront that fear and overcome it. It's a matter of helping your mate rise above his fear, to a pedestal that gives him power over it.

One of the questions I always raise in premarital counseling is, "What do you plan to do about children?" A common indication of some degree of fear is the tendency to hedge the answer. The young man or woman may respond, "We'll decide about that later. We need to get to know each other first."

Unfortunately, one's attitude toward children is so crucial to a successful marriage relationship that it can't be put off. Certainly, you don't have to decide exactly when you'll have kids or even make a definite decision about whether you'll have them. But if spouses are not generally on the same wave length, storm clouds could be lurking on the marital horizon.

I've found that many couples don't want to lay their attitudes toward having children on the discussion table because they don't want to deal with deep-rooted fears. One person, if pushed, may admit, "I'd love to have children if I weren't afraid I'd get exhausted from hearing them cry all night and having to change their diapers."

Another may say, "Little kids may be okay, but I'm terrified of teenagers." Still another may confess, "I'd like to have a healthy child, but I'm scared to death of having one that might be deformed or disabled. I just don't think I could handle that." Also, a surprising number of young couples I run into worry that a child will cost too much; they want to spend their money on themselves, not on their offspring.

So it's important that you probe around, discover what your spouse's unspoken fears may be about children, and then work to free her from these fears. Otherwise, she, and your marriage as well, may begin to sink into a quagmire of anxieties.

Other fears that your mate may have could seem entirely personal to him, yet they may affect your marriage more than you'd expect. I know one man who enjoys airplanes so much that he took flying lessons and eventually became a very good private pilot. His wife, however, had a genuine fear of flying in small airplanes.

Interestingly enough, commercial airliners didn't bother her particularly. But she was terrified of small craft because she worried that the engine might konk out or the wind might cause the plane to crash during a take-off or landing. If you've ever ridden in a small one- or two-engine on a windy day and you don't know anything about flying, you can understand her fears. Sometimes, as the small plane swings back and forth on a landing approach, it seems that the pilot will never hit the runway.

This problem presented a fascinating situation to me for several reasons. First of all, I'm a pilot myself and I wanted to help the woman understand something about the safety features of flying in a small plane. At the same time, I saw an opportunity for both spouses to put their mates on a pedestal.

You see, the husband had an opportunity to respect his wife's anxieties and to help her overcome her fears, perhaps by subordinating or even relinquishing his own interests as a pilot. At the same time, the wife was confronted with a chance to master her fears so that her husband's desire to fly could be satisfied.

The solution they arrived at was a compromise that satisfied both and at the same time allowed both to grow personally. The basic approach we used was for the three of us to sit down and spend some time talking about the nuts and bolts of airplanes. I shared some of my experiences in the air and supplied her with literature showing the protective features and safety record of her husband's plane.

Because she *wanted* to please her husband and put his hobby above her fears, she began to make steady progress. Gradually, this wife just gave up her fear. She made up her mind to trust her husband as a pilot and to let go of the fear for the sake of her marriage.

In her mind, she said (and prayed), "I'm trusting my husband and God to take care of me, instead of giving in to this fear."

For his part, the husband bided his time as his wife struggled to adjust to life with a pilot. He actually cut down on his flying hours significantly so that he could be with her more. Gradually, though, as she got acclimated to flying and actually began to get a kick out of it, they increased their time in the air. And they found that they were able to increase their ability to go on exciting weekend jaunts and family vacations. Now they have a little two-seater sports plane that they enjoy flying as a pastime together.

Certainly, although living with fear in a marriage is a strain on both partners, neither should *demand* that the other give up a fear. That just won't work. Rather, the person without the fear should pitch in and patiently help his partner reduce the impact of those fears. John declared in the New Testament, "There is no fear in love, but perfect love casts out fear" (1 John 4:18, RSV). That's the kind of love you have to show your own mate if you hope to help her rise above the most debilitating fears that undermine marriages.

Building Block #7: Forgive and forget.
Although I've placed this building block in seventh place, it may be the most important of all. There are many little wounds that spouses inflict on each other and on the marriage relationship over time. Often, sadly, no effort is made to heal them. They just lie open and festering over months and years, waiting to be pricked and sliced again and again.

The greatest salve I know for these hurts and harms is the simple act of seeking forgiveness. If you fly off the handle at your wife or unjustly accuse your husband of something, the most effective way to repair the emotional and spiritual damage is just to say, "I'm sorry."

But simple as this act is, it's very difficult to do, mainly because we know asking forgiveness automatically makes us vulnerable. You may very well say, "I'm sorry," and the immediate response could be, "I'll say you are, and you'd better not do it again!" Or more commonly, a spouse may reply, "Well, it's easy to say you're sorry, but that doesn't undo all the damage."

Despite the danger that the act of asking for forgiveness won't be generously received, it's important to make the effort. In fact, the key thing is the effort; it's a mistake even to worry about eliciting a perfect forgiving response. You see, there's something exceedingly powerful in simply seeking forgiveness, in just saying you're sorry. That sets certain spiritual forces into motion, and even if the desired response isn't forthcoming at first, eventually the beneficial payoff will come in your relationship. Believe me, it will!

We all lose our tempers on occasion and say things that

hurt the feelings of others. We also forget birthdays and innumerable other special occasions that are important to our partners. But regardless of the response you expect or get, there is one very good rule of thumb to follow: Never hesitate to be the first to apologize and say you're sorry.

By asking for forgiveness, you're demonstrating that you respect your mate and that you place the highest value on peace and justice within the relationship. In fact, you're showing symbolically that you're willing to take your hat off, get down on your knees, and admit you're wrong. You're actually saying, "I'm willing to beg—beg your forgiveness!" It's hard for a proud person to show he's more serious than that.

The prophet Jeremiah quoted the Lord as making this startling statement: "I will forgive their iniquity, and I will remember their sin no more" (Jeremiah 31:34). Forgive and forget—that's the divine model, and it should be a guide for us as well. The act of asking for and accepting forgiveness should be the final and ultimate "cleanser" for hurtful or intentional mistakes in a relationship. Damage may have been done, but it's imperative that it be repaired as soon as possible.

". . . [D]o not let the sun go down on your anger," says the apostle Paul. That means if you've exploded at your spouse, you've got to do your best to clear the air before bedtime. Any bitter or injured feelings that linger until the next day are just going to fester and cause further infection. Forgiveness is the healing force that has the power to repair any rift in your pedestal relationship.

Building Block #8: Communicate with a clean mouth.
Now, for the final three building blocks, I'm going to get on a rather old-fashioned high horse. The very notion of putting your mate on a pedestal somehow seems outdated on its face, so you're already aware that I'm drawing on values whose roots run deeper than just the past ten years of the twentieth century. Now, you're about to find out just what a Neanderthal I am.

First of all, I'm convinced that the degree of respect you have for your spouse comes across in the way you speak. I realize that four-letter words and profane remarks are so commonplace these days that they have become socially acceptable in many quarters. When a husband or wife gets angry, it's often *expected* that a flow of four-letter words will issue forth. And even when calm, casual conversations are involved, the language may get just as dirty.

That indeed may be the nature of our society. But I'm old-fashioned and square enough to believe that profanity and cursing shouldn't be tolerated within the home. In working with various couples, I've found a correlation between such talk and a destructive undercutting of the relationship. A foul mouth is poisonous to the respect and love that undergird a marriage.

In part, the poison comes from certain assumptions that lie, consciously or subconsciously, behind the bad language. Some may argue that using earthy phrases helps people relax and even enhances intimacy. But at the same time, profanity lowers the level of the conversation. When you use a four-letter word in the presence of your spouse, you're saying, "We can communicate better in a gutter than we can on a mountaintop." You're also doing the opposite of raising the position of your mate; you're forcing her to interact with you on a plane far below the pedestal of respect that she deserves and which a strong, tough marriage demands.

And there's more. There's a darker side to this whole question of language, which I'm firmly convinced is the most insidious dimension of all. There's something about profanity that carries a curse quality. When you use the name of God or one of the heavenly (or demonic) beings in casual talk, you're invoking powers that go far beyond our meager human strength. As you know, cursing may actually involve calling on God or another divine being to send down evil or injury to someone else. There's a definite spiritual power in oaths and condemnations.

Of course, you may be thinking by now, "This guy is a little weird. After all, in my circle of friends, a little profanity is considered sophisticated. And it doesn't have any more power than a hiccup."

But don't reject what I'm saying so quickly. Even when used in jest, a word of profanity or a curse possesses a certain locomotion of its own, a spiritual power for evil. When you hit your spouse with a bad word, he may smile at the time. But that word stays with him. It seeps down into his self-concept and becomes part of his identity. Also, the profanity pulls him down to a lower level in the marriage than he deserves. So keep your dialogue clean and healthy—as preventive maintenance for your spouse's pedestal.

Building Block #9: *Show chivalry.*
Now I'm *really* getting old-fashioned! After all, in this age of women's rights, chivalry is dead, isn't it?

My answer is an emphatic *no!* First of all, in the broadest sense, chivalry isn't limited to some outmoded notion of medieval knighthood. Even today, the tradition of chivalry charges on as an attitude marked by fairness, generosity, honor, and kindness to others.

Many times, the chivalrous action is just a brief respectful or supportive gesture. When I open a door for my wife or help her with her coat, the symbolic message is: I care for you. Or as I hold an umbrella for her and gently cradle her arm as we cross a slippery street, she knows I'm not implying that she can't do all that by herself. Rather, she understands I'm showing her through a simple action that I hold her in high esteem. She is the most important woman in my life.

Also, even though chivalry was often associated in the past with the way men showed special courtesies to women so that they were raised up on a kind of pedestal, I believe the term should also apply to the way women treat men. So a wife might tell her husband how young or handsome he looks. Or she might compliment him on how well he conducted himself at a business gathering. As she strokes his ego in these small ways, she is paving the way for a much broader impact that will benefit her marriage.

Finally, as these small, gallant gestures are traded back and forth, they should be accepted in the same spirit and respect in which they are given. I know one woman who typically got flustered when her husband romanced her with a compliment or a public kiss. She tended to brush him off or even make fun of his efforts, and eventually he stopped trying to be chivalrous. This was the first step in a growing distance that developed between them and threatened to cause serious problems in their marriage.

So return the compliment or the gallant gesture with grace and class. A smile, a gentle squeeze, or a simple "thank you" is often all that's required. But when you receive in the same spirit that your spouse gives, you'll find you're mutually lifting one another up and establishing the firmest possible foundation for your marriage.

Building Block #10: Be ready to raise a wall of protection. One of the great things about marriage is that there are now two of you to face the slings and arrows of the world and not just one. In fact, if God is a part of your relationship, there are more than two. It's like the difference between trying to play a quarter of football against the Pittsburgh Steelers all by yourself and having a double line of Dallas Cowboys leading interference for you.

One of the most common ways this principle comes into play occurs during social gatherings. When a husband and wife are with other people, the spouses sometimes vie with one another for the floor, especially if one thinks he can tell a funny family story better than the other. Or all too often there's a tendency on the part of one partner to belittle the other.

I recall one man who fancied himself an expert on the artistic value of movies. When his wife would offer a comment on a film they had both seen, he would invariably attack her judgment: "Oh, Laura, you just don't understand acting." Or, "What you're missing there, Laura, is the significance of the editing."

Finally, Laura began to lapse into silences when such discussions arose, and she began to participate less and less in conversations on other topics. Her resentment against her husband grew, until finally they had to seek counseling to work their problems out.

The better approach here, and one the couple began to use, is what I call "protecting the conversation." This is a kind of art form in itself and requires a great deal of patience, politeness, and respect to work. The main idea is to try to shape and mold a group discussion so that your mate feels comfortable and is even given an opportunity to shine in public. Here are some examples:

- When your spouse says something that seems a little off the mark, instead of being the first to criticize, jump in and expand on the statement so that it makes more sense.
- If your husband or wife is being left out of a general discussion, see to it that he or she is included.
- If your mate is clearly uncomfortable with the subject at hand, try to change it.
- If your spouse is quite knowledgeable on a particular topic that hasn't been discussed, ask a question that will allow her to make a comment of real interest to the group.

There are countless other examples I can think of, but I think you get the idea. And just remember: It's a hard, cruel world out there, so what's the point in trying to face it alone? Start operating as a team, and you'll find the two of you can put together many winning combinations as you face the challenges of life.

So these are the ten building blocks that I've found can provide the firmest foundation for your mate's pedestal. Strengthening your spouse's position in each of these areas will raise him up to a level of confidence and personal power that would be impossible without your help.

If your love is genuine and deep, it should be satisfying just to know you've helped your mate rise to greater levels of happiness and achievement. But there are also broader benefits that may bolster your marriage and you personally.

First of all, I've discovered a common principle that might be stated like this: The quality of a marriage tends to improve as the self-confidence or level of achievement of one partner improves. The only exception I can think of to this principle would be when competition between the spouses becomes a factor. That is, if you start becoming a very "classy," successful person, your mate might begin to resent the elevation in your status because you seem to be "getting ahead" of him. But if you're the one who is largely responsible for your spouse's personal improvement, your reaction is more likely to be prideful than competitive.

A second principle that has impressed me is that as you help push and prop your spouse to higher planes of self-esteem, many benefits are going to come sliding right back down to you. Of course, your motive can't be to give in order to get. But there seems to be a rule of reciprocity that runs deep in the nature of the universe, a precept that can be best summed up in the words of Jesus in Luke 6:38: ". . . give, and it will be given to you; good measure, pressed down, shaken together, running over, will be put into your lap. For the measure you give will be the measure you get back." (RSV)

So the foundation you're building for your loved one will support much more than just one person. Provide a pedestal for your mate, and you'll provide one for yourself and your relationship as well. That's the law and the prophetic word, the essence of the first commandment of a tough marriage.

THE SECOND COMMANDMENT

Kiss Mom and Dad Goodbye

There is a natural order to life that begins and ends with being a parent. We're born, we grow up, we leave home. Next, we marry, start our own homes, and have our own children. Then the cycle begins anew.

But even in this natural flow of things, one crucial event must occur if we want to ensure that family life will continue smoothly from generation to generation. That's the time when we cut the emotional umbilical cord and say a fond farewell to our parents. It's when we actually and symbolically "kiss Mom and Dad goodbye" and begin our lives as independent adults.

In other words, every tough, durable marriage is characterized by substantial independence from parents and in-laws. I'm not suggesting that it's necessary to cut all ties with old Mom and Dad—far from it! Rather, a couple must reaffirm the love for parents and then move ahead and concentrate most of their attention on building up their own relationship.

This fundamental principle has been operative since the dawn of human history, and it has been etched permanently into the philosophical and religious fabric of civilization. Genesis 2:24 states the idea perhaps best of all: "A man leaves his father and mother and cleaves to his wife."

But oh, that the launching of new marriage and family relationships were always a simple event! The dilemma posed by the final goodbye presents families with at least two hard issues.

On the one hand, many children have great difficulty leaving home. The comfortable nest created by a mother or father can make the responsibilities and risks of the outside world seem highly unattractive. On the other hand, many parents resist letting their children go. They play on the devotion and love of their offspring to keep them around well beyond an age when one should be striking out into the world and starting an independent family.

So leaving the comfortable cocoon of childhood is certainly not inevitable or automatic. Recently, a woman who is a top executive for a large cosmetics company told me this story. She's about fifty years old now and has been married since she was twenty. But don't let the length of her marriage fool you! It was so tough at first for her husband to cut his emotional ties to his mother that the strain almost wrecked their marriage.

During the early years of the marriage, the husband made no bones about his loyalty to and admiration for his mother. In fact, he openly admitted that he felt he owed more than he could ever repay to his mother. His actions also suggested that his allegiance to his mother came first, before the interests of his wife and their young daughter. Naturally, the wife was hurt, especially when it became evident that she and their child were playing second fiddle.

For example, when it came to a choice between the husband spending time with his mother or with his wife and daughter on weekends, his mother always won out. Also, when the time came for family vacations, they always went to the mother's home or to the resort she knew best. The wife had very little voice in these family decisions: it was mother and son, not husband and wife.

Obviously, for a woman with the strong personality and deep sense of justice of this executive wife, this arrangement was hard to tolerate. She finally sat down with her husband, explained that she had reached the end of her rope, and informed him in the strongest terms possible that things had to change.

Fortunately, he got the message. Sometimes, the ties from the old homestead are so strong that a husband or wife simply can't cut the apron strings. In such a situation, the marriage gets kissed goodbye. But this husband knew the riot act was being read to him, even if in a gentle way.

So he immediately started making adjustments in his relationship with his mother. He didn't sever his relationship with her, but he did take the advice of a counselor and devoted a solid month to being only with his wife and daughter during his free time. Then he started working his mother back into his family's life. But he made sure that the plans he had made for his wife and daughter received his priority.

This family relationship worked out rather nicely, with all parties eventually getting on good terms. The wife and her mother-in-law eventually even grew close to one another. But too often in such situations the problems run so deep that extensive marriage or psychological counseling may be needed to work through the "letting go" of Mom or Dad—not to mention the prodigious patience on the part of the spouse who is competing with Mom or Dad.

Sometimes, the most fundamental challenge is for a person just to recognize that he can't marry his mother or father. Unconsciously, he may carry into marriage an ideal image of the mate, which conforms to that of an admired parent. The problem is that no spouse can live up to an idealized version of anyone, and especially not of a parent. So if you can just get your preconceptions about what you want from your spouse and marriage out on the table and begin to discuss them with one another, you're already halfway to the solution of most problems.

In the best of all possible worlds, parents should take the initiative early to train their children to "leave the nest." As children, we begin to establish a sense of independence when we take our first steps as toddlers. This separation from parental influence continues as we begin to play with neighborhood children and then spend increasing amounts of time in the company of our peers in school. A sense of special identity as an individual should grow steadily as we get older, and in time we develop the emotional capacity to separate from our parents' family and to embark on our own domestic adventure.

The act of leaving your parents, of kissing them goodbye, is one of those ultimate steps toward maturity that you must take if you hope to realize the full potential of a marriage. But don't get the wrong idea: We're not talking about rejection of your parents. We're talking about maturity for everyone—parents and children alike. This maturity, which involves much more than just getting older, is the means of entering into a deeper adult relationship between parents and children. The warm affection and high regard you have for your parents can become the cornerstone for a new adult-to-adult relationship rather than a perpetually stunted child-to-parent scenario.

But sometimes, one or both partners in a marriage relationship just can't seem to put childhood behind. That "goodbye kiss," which seals the end of the era of immaturity and opens the door to full adulthood, just doesn't connect. Why?

In my counseling and research, I've identified at least six resistance points that make it hard for people who fail to say *sayonara* to their old parental ties. Some relate primarily to faults in the parents and some relate to difficulties in adult, married children. Any can sound the death knell of a marriage if it gets out of hand. At the same time, all these resistance points can be eliminated if one party or the other takes the initiative to break through the emotional barriers and bid a mature farewell to old ties.

Resistance #1: You don't want to release the security and comfort of the good life at home.
Let's face it, not all people have had a horrendous childhood! Not all adults have had to live through the terror of child abuse or some sort of "Cinderella syndrome," involving rejection by parents and siblings! In other words, it's natural that many people have enjoyed their family relationships as kids. But the good life at home may make them more dependent on the old home ties than anyone realizes.

I know one young wife who spent most of each day at her mother's home, which was in the same neighborhood. She ate with her mother, spent most of the afternoon visiting with her, and eventually began taking home-cooked meals back to her husband in the evenings.

Clearly, this was a secure sort of arrangement for the young wife that continued her childhood dependence on her family. But understandably, her mother began to get weary of the extra cooking and the constant presence of her daughter. For one thing, the daughter was getting in the way of the older woman's own social life. Finally, the straw that broke the camel's back came when the daughter began to quote out of context to her husband various remarks her mother had made about what the young couple might do to improve their relationship. The husband hit the ceiling at what he interpreted as unfair and unsolicited criticism. Also, the mother was incensed that she hadn't been quoted accurately and had been misunderstood.

Things went from bad to worse, until the couple finally had the good sense to seek help from a professional counselor. After just one session, this objective observer was able to sort out the various issues and make some practical suggestions that made everyone happier almost immediately.

The adjustment was very simple: The young woman stopped spending so much time at her mother's home. Although the wife was not oriented toward the job market, she did get involved in volunteer work and actually began to make a significant contribution to needy people in her community. Just by distancing herself a little from her mother, she found the relationships in that triangle got noticeably better.

So obviously, having your everyday physical and emotional needs met for a time as a young adult isn't a good reason for you to plan to rely on the security of your parents' home to provide the security in your marriage. Eventually, you'll find your welcome wearing thin as your parents near retirement age. Or you'll sense, quite appropriately, that your own development as a person can't go any further without your venturing forth on your own.

By not taking responsibility for your own welfare, you force your parents to become more like God than an earthly mother or father can be. Your folks are thrust into a role of perpetual care, and you slip into childish dependence rather than growing up emotionally and spiritually.

Resistance #2:   Your parents have "scared" you about what a cold, cruel world lies in wait outside the home.
Perhaps Mom and Dad were just trying to be helpful when they elaborated on how tough it is to make a living. They may honestly have believed they were preparing you properly for the difficult times that lay ahead.

But sometimes, the end result of such an approach is that the parents generate negative feelings and frustrations in the child. They may really mean to be offering constructive advice when they say something like, "You can't possibly manage everything on your own . . . you have no idea how hard it is to make ends meet . . . how can you make enough to pay the rent and meet your car payments?"

But what the child hears in such remarks is: I'm inadequate to cope with the real world. It'll be pure luck if I'm able to make a go of it on my own. I won't even survive by myself!

Much parental prattle about hard times ahead will frighten a child. This kind of talk undermines the child's confidence and self-esteem. After all, what child wants to grow up to face such an undesirable world? Better just to hang around the house and never grow up. That's far less threatening, despite the fact the child may have to deal with negative-minded parents posing as economic guardian angels. But neither children nor parents will ever grow up if this attitude of the helpless child is allowed to continue.

A good antidote to this particular resistance point is to conduct a "reality check." If you find yourself in the position of the frightened adult "child," take a good, hard look about whether your fears are justified.

For example, examine your parents' motives. Perhaps their dire warnings about the economic and social disasters that await you just reflect their own selfish effort to make themselves feel important and powerful. Sure it's a tough world out there. But there are also plenty of opportunities for success and excitement. The problem is that achievement will be impossible if those apron strings remain uncut.

Then, take a look at what your fears are doing to your marriage. Most likely, that all-important relationship has been suffering because of your fears of a scary future. Your spouse is probably quite frustrated with the unhealthy hold your parents' attitudes have on you. Because of this frustration, your strongest support for breaking free of your fears will come from your spouse. She undoubtedly wants you to become bolder and more independent; it's in her self-interest and in the best interests of the marriage.

So talk things out with your mate. Then formulate a practical plan to break free of the "goblins" in your imagination. Finally, rely on your spouse for support as you take those first tentative steps toward a tougher marriage that can fly on its own and has its own nest.

Resistance #3: *You resent your folks because they "kicked you out" of their home.*

In this case, your ties may have been severed with your parents, but they are the ones who took the initiative and pushed you away. As a result, you probably harbor some bitter feelings towards them.

Sometimes, parents do resent their children. Despite the joy that a youngster can bring into the home, parents may allow the negative factors to crowd out the positive relations. For example, the family may have been financially pinched, and one or both parents tended constantly to "look over their shoulder" and imagine how easy things might have been without the added expense of one or more children.

You'll recall that even Mr. Darling in J. M. Barrie's *Peter Pan* questioned keeping his eldest child, Wendy:

"For a week or two after Wendy came it was doubtful whether they would be able to keep her, as she was another mouth to feed. Mr. Darling was frightfully proud of her, but he was very honourable, and he sat on the edge of Mrs. Darling's bed, holding her hand and calculating expenses, while she looked at him imploringly. She wanted to risk it, come what might, but that was not his way; his way was with a pencil and a piece of paper. . . ."

Mr. Darling relented, of course. Wendy stayed; and he became a devoted if somewhat eccentric father. But that may not have been quite the situation in your home. Perhaps you stayed at home, but you got the sense that your parents couldn't wait to get rid of you. And when you did get old enough to fend for yourself, they made it clear that you were expected to venture forth on your own—*immediately!*

If your experience has been something like this, it's important to try to understand your parents, to "get inside their heads" and see exactly what makes them tick. When you begin to explore their attitudes, you'll undoubtedly find that the problem isn't with you; it's with them.

In analyzing their situation, many adult offspring have discovered that their parents have become caught up in their own immaturity and self-centeredness. They are sometimes not even aware of how to fulfill the nurturing role required to prepare their children for mature independence. Also, they may be oblivious to the fact that it's sometimes necessary to prolong the transition of the child's departure from home. Some young people need extra help to "fly" on their own.

Impatient, immature parents who can't wait to be free of a daughter may encourage her to get involved in an early marriage. Or a son may be shipped off to boarding school while still so young that his fledgling value system hasn't fully developed. Or parents might encourage a teenage boy to enlist in the military, to "grow up" or to "learn real discipline." Too often, these departures are "angry leavings." They may well occur impulsively, as a result of a family argument. The bottom line is declared in no uncertain terms: Get out!

That's a tough farewell for any youngster and certainly a far cry from a goodbye kiss. Children in such circumstances carry this burden of rejection around with them for a long time, and maybe even for their entire lives. They often interpret the parental message as: I'm not worthy of being loved. That can give rise to emotional problems that reach far beyond an unpleasant parting from home.

I'd like to go even one step further. I think that one reason for the high rate of teenage suicide may be that some youngsters take these rejections from parents too much to heart. They think, "The people who brought me into this world now want to get rid of me, so I must be totally worthless. They don't care if I live or die, and I don't care either!"

In any case, there is bound to be anger, fear, frustration, and resentment when children are kicked out of the house. It's difficult, if not impossible, for abandoned, unloved young people to make a truly successful, contented married life for themselves. Even if such a child makes it to the top of his field, there is almost always some serious problem stemming from childhood that he carries along as excess emotional baggage.

So if you find yourself in this situation, take a mental step back and try to understand what made your parents behave as they did. Then you'll be in a much better position to understand yourself.

Resistance #4: You were a rebel who is convinced, My parents failed me!
Many young people leave home in rebellion because they are disappointed in their parents. Over the years, I've come into contact with a number of young adults, many in their twenties, who are unable or unwilling to make a commitment—and this includes a long-term tie to their own mates, who are bearing the brunt of the rebel's instability. The rebels tend to have a long history of failure, whether in romance, business, or purely personal goals. And who do they blame for their misfortunes? Their parents, of course.
Stock excuses range from one extreme to another:

- I grew up without any love from my mom and dad.
- They loved my older sister most and gave her all the advantages.
- They programmed me for failure by making me believe there's no way I could improve myself.
- My parents were failures in their careers (or marriage) and I'm destined to repeat their unhappiness.

When the going gets tough and disappointments come one after the other, these young people usually point an accusing finger at their folks rather than take a good close look at themselves. They seem to have a sense of anger, powerlessness, and inevitability in the face of major challenges. Instead of looking for a solution or an escape route, they give up far too easily. Everything looks impossible to them.
Some of these youngsters also become afraid that they will repeat the mistakes their parents made. They don't like what they see in their parents and they'd prefer to take a different route in their lives. That's the reason they rejected their folks.

But their own low self-esteem takes the heart out of any effort they may make to head in a different direction. When things become difficult, they throw up their hands and say, "It's just in the genes." Like lemmings, they move inexorably toward a repetition of the errors made by Mom and Dad. The sense of the inevitability of their lives makes them grow more and more hostile to their parents. They seem to feed on their misfortunes.

If this description fits you, take heart! It's possible to exert more control over your life if you'll just tackle the problem step by step. The first question to ask is, "What can I do?" If you can get to this point, then you'll start assuming that it's *possible* to do something. That means that half your battle is won.

Then I tell the person, "Now, you've got to face your past, accept it, and even *bless* it." A "blessing" in Old and New Testament understanding is a bestowal of good through a spiritually powerful set of words or actions. One way to bestow such good would be to pray that you'll understand your past and your parents better. You might also ask God to improve your relationship with your mother and father.

At the same time, you can invoke a kind of blessing on your past by recognizing: My past is part of me. I can't change it. But I can *learn* from it. In fact, if I go about this the right way, I think I can become an even stronger person *because* of my past.

Those "can do" people who have successfully risen above such difficulties are more likely than many others to exercise power over hard challenges. Once you've mastered the control your past has over you, you'll become increasingly confident that you can master other problems as well.

One woman I know found that she was stymied in moving ahead in her job and in overcoming problems in her marriage. To explain her problems, she always tended to fall back on the lame excuse, "My parents failed me."

That was the perfect alibi, or so she thought, for experiencing a string of failures for the rest of her life. But then she learned that her husband was getting so frustrated with her that he was on the verge of walking out. She knew she had to do something fast if she wanted to rescue what remained of her marriage.

When we sat down to talk about her problem, it became evident that even though her parents had been rather stern and lacked understanding at times, she had also been at fault. She had given up on them in frustration, left home for good at age sixteen, and still harbored deep resentment toward them.

I encouraged her to stop and think about what she was really saying to herself. She was assuming, I said, "My parents' behavior has predetermined who and what I am."

Then I asked her, "Tell me, do you think there is any such thing as free will? Do you think you can exercise any control at all over your own future?"

She answered yes, she did think she had some freedom and control over her life. She also admitted that she had been at least partially at fault in the rupture in the relationship with her mother and father. They were strong-willed, but so was she. She had wanted to live her life her own way while she was still under their roof, and they had refused to put up with such an arrangement. The final result was that she pulled out of her home in a huff.

As we chatted further, I got her to consider which would be the better course for her to take: On the one hand, she could continue to cling to her present attitude that failure with her husband and with life in general was inevitable. That, I pointed out, was the childish, immature, fatalistic view of the world. Or she could try to change things. She could recognize that not only did she have free will; she could also make use of it. There was naturally some chance that she would fail in her effort to change her life. But would it be better to sit tight and be sure of failure or venture forth and perhaps succeed in transforming her entire existence for the better?

In this case, the woman agreed to try. Gradually, over a period of months, she saw significant progress in her relationship with her husband and also in her ability to deal with her past. The rebellious spirit that had gripped her as a teenager and had threatened to rip apart her marriage faded away. But this doesn't always happen, of course. Unfortunately, some people take the other route: They choose to become more childish. The thirty- or forty-year-old who constantly whines about parents is unattractive at best and self-destructive at worst. Staging a "pity party" over childhood disappointments only aggravates underlying anger. What's needed instead is to bless both one's past and parents. Only by taking this step can you hope to find the motivation to move ahead and benefit from the future.

Resistance #5: *Mom and Dad play the guilt game by saying, "We need you!"*
This is a real toughie for those who are trying to bid their parents goodbye in a mature, constructive way. It's especially hard if you find yourself making a valuable contribution to your family's living arrangements. Some parents, especially those who are widowed, may actually overextend themselves financially on purpose so that they can beg you back home with cries of "family responsibility!" Other times, they may not insist that you come live with them; they just want you to provide a financial net or supplement for their own income.

I've heard a number of parents say to their children, "We just bought this piece of farm equipment . . . or a new car . . . or carpeting for the house, and we need you to help pay the bills." Then they subtly work on the child's conscience and sense of responsibility. It's the old guilt game. They may remind you how much it cost to put you through college and then leave you with the unspoken thought, And so, dear, don't you think a little repayment is now due?

Many times, young people will respond and begin to help their parents out in such situations. It's hard to be genuinely fond of parents who use such ruthless tactics. It's also dangerous to your own marriage relationship, because it's likely your spouse will get impatient with your unwise use of your money and may also begin to regard you as weak.

So what can you do if you find yourself in such an uncomfortable spot?

Being a very practical person, I tend to rely first on a hardnosed, dollars-and-cents analysis. If your parents are asking you for money, it's your right—in fact, your responsibility, since you have your own household to think about—to ask for an accounting. That is, get Mom to lay out her personal budget so you can evaluate it. If it becomes evident that she is getting more from insurance, pensions, and Social Security benefits than you earn from your job, then your decision becomes easier. Even if she makes less than you do, as will usually be the case, her basic expenses may be so low that she has more spendable income than you do.

Such an analysis should show you if there is real financial need; and if there is, you will want to respond. But in the course of chatting with her about her finances, you may well find she doesn't want your money at all. She just wants more of you. Perhaps you can accommodate her needs without jeopardizing the needs of your own family. In any case, a heart-to-heart talk with Mom or Dad will probably do far more good than immediately caving in to initial demands.

Finally, always be sensitive. Sometimes, the requests may be the desperate cry of a lonely old person who is dying inside because of a lack of sufficient warm human contact. I'm reminded of one aged grandmother who had been placed in a nursing home but then went steadily downhill emotionally, physically, and spiritually. The reason, I believe, was that she rarely received any visits from family members. Her cries for help, like the wails of a baby who never receives a response, finally ceased. But the need was still there.

Then, for some reason, it dawned on one of her grandchildren that the old woman needed someone around who really cared for her. So the girl began to pay visits to the nursing home. Gradually, the grandmother recovered somewhat and actually began to enjoy some of those long-lost personal and familial ties just before her death.

Clearly, a cry of help from a parent presents a difficult, primordial issue for any adult child. The duty to render mature, balanced judgments about how to express true love has now shifted to the son or daughter. The child has now become the parent, and the burden can sometimes seem too heavy to bear. But as you reflect back on what your parents did for you in your childhood, the responsibility may seem more manageable and understandable.

Resistance #6:   An overindulgent mom or dad can undercut your independence.
This is the other side of the coin. In the last section, we considered the parent who cries out for help or clings to the adult child for real or imagined succoring. But what about the parent who showers the adult child with gifts in an effort to "buy" that child's continued dependence?

The overindulgence may stem from such causes as:

- a misguided sense of the child's needs;
- an attempt to compensate for love the parent thinks the child may have been deprived of;
- an effort in a broken home to make up for unhappiness and stress the child may have suffered; or
- a means of "keeping the child quiet."
- a "guilt offering" by parents who worry that their discipline tactics are too harsh and that the children will hate and reject them.

These attempts to pay off a youngster may begin at an early age and continue well up into adulthood. Basically, I believe that such parents are afraid their children will reject them if they refuse certain things. As for the adult child, it may be easy and tempting just to hold out an open palm and wait for those attractive handouts.

A less neurotic but still questionable reason for indulging a child well up into adulthood came out recently in one counseling session I conducted. An older parent, who still had a thirty-year-old son by the umbilical cord, said: "I really had it tough when I was growing up, and I made up my mind long ago to make it easier for my kids. I saw that they had a good education, a car, and all the money they wanted. And I'll continue to give them help as long as they need me."

This parent had insisted on setting up his son in business and also on buying him a home. So the younger fellow grew up without confidence in his own abilities and without experiencing satisfaction in his own achievements. Everything had been provided for him. Consequently, he wasn't sure he could make it on his own. He just kept accepting the continual flow of gifts without lifting a finger to protest.

Underneath it all, this pampered young man had become profoundly dependent on his parents. When he finally understood that he was going to have to make a go of life on his own, it came as a shock. It took a year or two for him to recover his equilibrium and begin the process of learning to survive on his own in the world. Although such parents may have the best of intentions, they deprive their child of the opportunity to grow up. Mom and Dad may think they are just being generous. But in truth, they are creating children who lack the capacity and toughness to make a success of life in general or marriage in particular.

One overzealous woman I know really roused her son-in-law's anger and almost jeopardized her daughter's marriage with such overindulgence. She had never liked the idea of "losing" her daughter, and so she had refused to let go, either emotionally or financially.

Long after the young couple had been married, the mother continued to buy extravagant gifts for her daughter. There were designer clothes, antique furniture, and many other luxuries that most couples just starting out can't afford.

At first, the husband didn't seem to object. But his resentment began to fester, and it finally climaxed when their first baby was born. The expectant grandmother had already purchased all the nursery furnishings, and she couldn't wait to pamper her new granddaughter with more gifts. But when she arrived at the hospital with a bulging shopping bag in tow, that was too much for her son-in-law.

"This baby is *my* first child, and I think I can provide for her needs myself!" he shouted.

Granted, this may have been an overreaction to one shopping bag full of clothes. But when you consider all that had gone before, his outburst was just the tip of an emotional iceberg that had been accumulating for years.

Fortunately, the grandmother was a wise woman and she immediately realized her mistake. She had sensed she was being overly possessive, but since no one had called her on it, she had assumed her gifts were being accepted without any resentment. Obviously, as far as the son-in-law was concerned, that hadn't been the case. So she apologized profusely to her children, and her son-in-law apologized to her for his flash of anger. Soon, with the bad feelings having been thoroughly aired, the relationship could be rebuilt on a healthier, happier basis.

But another family situation didn't turn out quite so well. The mother and father supported their two able-bodied sons until they were well into their late twenties. These boys had gone off to college and graduated with flying colors. But after school, when they couldn't find jobs that paid enough to suit them, they simply refused to work.

Both got married, and they continued to live on handouts from their father, who was not a wealthy man. In fact, he had to get a second job to cover the extra expenses. From what I could tell, the father was afraid that the sons would turn against him if he refused to support them.

The tragedy here is that neither the young men nor their spouses had much respect for the parents. When grandchildren were born and the grandparents' money ran out, the young men of course had to get jobs. But they were ill-prepared, and it took divorces and several years of therapy before they finally "found themselves" and adjusted to the adult world.

How to Execute the Perfect Goodbye Kiss

Now you know some of the reasons, or the "resistances," if you will, that may have caused that goodbye kiss with your parents to fail to connect. Still, if you hope to pursue your own marriage with no untidy strings attached, it's essential that you bid your parents a firm, loving, and complete farewell. And quite frankly, the burden rests on you to take the initiative.

The first step in executing an effective goodbye kiss is to recognize that you simply can't look out for a spouse and a parent on equal terms. At the same time, however, you can help your parents to make an appropriate adjustment to your new independence. Perhaps the most effective way to reassure insecure parents is to talk openly with them about their fears. Then, to confirm your love, it's sometimes helpful to bestow on them a simple gesture of honor and respect. That may be a small gift, with a note of thanks for all that they mean to you. Or you might take them out to dinner in a nice restaurant. You might even throw a party for them to celebrate a wedding anniversary or birthday.

There's no set formula that works for every family. But any of these special gestures say: You are still a part of my life, and I love you very much. A special gift or celebration can also provide a time to muse together about how a new phase of life—your own marriage—has begun and how important that is to the continuation of family ties and traditions.

The basic message you want to convey is: I'm grown-up now. I'm following a normal pattern by living away from home with my spouse. I still love you, Mom and Dad. And this new stage in our relationship simply makes it possible for even *more* people, including my spouse and children, to love you.

It may take a number of conversations before you and your parents really get on the same wave length. But if you keep at it, you'll succeed in getting the message across. As you talk, give them credit where credit is due. Then, embrace them in a real-life hug and kiss. You now have the freedom to commit your strongest affections to a new relationship, which demands intense loyalties of its own.

Also, by moving beyond your childhood, you help ensure that you won't make your mate a substitute parent. Once you commit yourself to marriage, there should be no looking back wistfully toward home. You mustn't constantly compare what you had with your parents to what you have now with your spouse. Your past will always be with you, but it's important to build on it, not be stifled by it. Married life is supposed to be different! If you kiss Mom and Dad this sort of final goodbye and embrace married life with enthusiasm for what it can bring, you'll actually be blessing all that has been and honoring all that will be.

THE THIRD COMMANDMENT

Speak the Truth in Love

"The honeymoon is over!"

I've heard those words thousands of times through my years of counseling, and they usually indicate the same thing: A couple's first big argument has exploded on the peaceful meadows of matrimonial bliss.

The fight has usually arisen out of some petty misunderstanding or disagreement, and more often than not, it can be resolved rather easily. But it signals a rude awakening as to what the real world of marriage is all about. They have to "wake up and smell the coffee," as the old country saying goes. At some point, you have to rise from your bed of roses and recognize that the floor is cold, your teeth need brushing, and there are bound to be some bad moods, hard words, and bitter conflicts.

After all, no matter how much two people seem to be alike, each comes to the marriage with a wealth of different habits, expectations, values, and feelings. When you tie the knot, you become one in many ways, but at the same time, on another level you're still two separate human beings. What you are, down deep, can't possibly coincide exactly with what your spouse is. These differences—and also the simple fact that you're an individual with special needs and interests—make it inevitable that sooner or later, clashes are bound to occur. Oneness is both a fact and an ideal, but our individuality often intrudes to separate us when push comes to shove.

So it's vital for the survival of your marriage to realize at the outset that there will be disagreements. Such a realistic assessment will give you a sinewy substructure for subsequent efforts to deal with unpleasant encounters between you and your spouse.

Secondly, it's essential to understand that head-on verbal collisions with your mate may actually be healthy. Tough, straight talk can highlight areas that need adjustment. In other words, the true challenge lies not in looking for ways to avoid conflict. Rather, the important thing is to recognize a dispute for what it says about needs and weaknesses in your marriage. Then you're in a position to learn how to deal with all your difficulties more successfully.

Finally, even as you talk tough and straight, you have to do it gently, sensitively, and diplomatically. A tall order? Sure! But building any great marriage is a tall order. If you do it step by step and bring all your personal and spiritual resources to bear on your problems, you have to come out on top. That's one of the basic principles of the universe!

But now, let's get down to brass tacks on this issue of the tough but effective language of marriage. The basic approach to resolving any marital problem can best be summed up in the words of the apostle Paul, who urged upon the church at Ephesus the practice of "speaking the truth in love" (Ephesians 4:15). There are many facets to this Pauline principle, but they are best seen in the light of two cardinal rules, which we'll now consider in some detail.

Cardinal Rule #1:   Start talking right now.
Most people wouldn't think of allowing cancer to fester in
the human body. Yet in a marriage relationship it's not un-
common for a couple to let problems go unresolved for
months or even years, with much the same effect as that of a
hideous malignant tumor.

As cancer spreads, it weakens the entire body, creating pain
and waste wherever it travels. Likewise, a marital conflict, if
unchecked, will inflict heartache and misery in a relationship
and poison the very lifeblood of the marriage. So when a conflict occurs, at least one partner needs to deal with it quickly
and thoroughly. Otherwise, the problem may go under-
ground and stay undetected for a time, only to resurface later
in more devastating ways.

I'm a firm believer in the biblical maxim "Be ye angry, and
sin not: let not the sun go down upon your wrath" (Ephesians
4:26). Recently, I counseled one man, "Never, never go to
bed while you're still angry with your spouse."

"Why?" he asked.

I pointed out the reason from his own experience. He and
his wife just couldn't seem to be around each other for more
than a few minutes without getting involved in an explosive
argument. The source of their problem could be traced back
more than a year in their relationship, to a practice they had
begun to follow because it was the easy way out, given the
fact they were such busy people.

You see, they would get into an argument and then turn
away from each other in bed and sulk until they fell asleep.
The morning bustle of getting ready for work always became a means of hiding from the source of the problem. Day
after day went by, and one matter after another was stirred
into the festering mix. Other priorities and demanding schedules prevented further confrontation for a time and added
to the silent, deep disease in the marriage. Finally, they
discovered there were so many unresolved conflicts that
they couldn't carry on a civil conversation with one another.

Inevitably, one of the spouses would resurrect one of the angry "loose ends" in their lives and hurl it as an insult toward the other.

In my conversations with them, I explained that conflict typically has a "snowball" quality that causes it to grow larger than life almost before you know what's happening. The result for the husband in this situation was anger, resentment, irritability, backbiting, hurt feelings, disappointment, quarrelsomeness—you name it. He was a prime representative of what might be called the aggressive personality in this conflict.

But there was also a passive side, which his wife reflected. Her hostility simmered, like the evil, bubbling caldron of *Macbeth*'s three "weird sisters." She became quiet, withdrawn, and distant, but with a decidedly mean and jagged edge to her silence.

Finally, the couple realized, Hey, we're not one entity anymore. We're two angry individuals fussing and attacking like cats and dogs. We don't even love each other!

At this point, it became difficult to identify the original grievance that had started this emotional cancer. The best I could do was to point out the *process* of wholehearted hostility that had entrapped them both.

Then I told them the only possible solution I saw: "Take your latest argument, your latest point of conflict, and resolve it! Don't go to sleep tonight until you've worked it out. Remember, when the next argument arises—and you can be sure it will—get on that immediately too!"

This couple is still whittling away at problems that began more than a year ago. But they're making headway, and that's what counts! Sometimes they find they just can't work out a solution before they fall asleep. But at least they make a start on it.

For example, one might say to the other, "I know that we don't agree on this situation. And quite frankly, I'm so tired, I can't think straight. But I do believe there *is* a way to work it out together. Why don't we talk about it more tomorrow night? How about over coffee after dinner?"

That's the healthy, tough way to handle things. You get the ball rolling and then make a specific appointment to wrap things up the next day. Also, this approach puts the problem in perspective. There's a tacit understanding that when the two of you tackle it together, you'll defeat it. You become a team again. You are two who have become one and are in the process of putting up a united front against the forces of dissension that want to pull you apart.

There are also other reasons to start working on the resolution of conflicts now rather than later. Certainly, your primary concern is your marriage. But at the same time, if things aren't going well in your marriage, the chances are they will start going sour outside your marriage as well. Relationships with friends or with colleagues at work will begin to become strained.

I know one woman who was under great stress from unresolved disputes at home, and that began to affect her job performance quite seriously. She became preoccupied with her marital concerns, and the result was sloppy work habits and displays of anger and impatience with her fellow workers. Her boss finally had to call her aside for a warning. It took several counseling sessions before she was able to trace her difficulties back to unresolved conflicts in her marriage.

Clearly, the infection of anger you've slept on can spread far beyond the bounds of your home life. So for your mutual benefit, it's wise to alert your spouse as soon as you detect a potential trouble spot. Airing your concerns immediately will help you vent pent-up frustration. Also, a quick injection of love and gentleness can defuse hostility and anxiety before they get out of hand.

One spouse may have to take the first step to resolving an argument or disagreement. But in the last analysis, it usually takes the best efforts of both to work through hostility and contention thoroughly. In any case, the first rule of speaking the truth in love is speed: Get started *now!*

Cardinal Rule #2:   Be truthful.
This may seem all too obvious, especially when a basic part of our third commandment is to "speak the truth." But I'm a great believer in belaboring the obvious when there's an important point to be made.

You see, the truth possesses explosive power, which can help you rebuild a rocky relationship in quick order. Yet this power can also be destructive if it's used the wrong way. Used the right way, though, it can purify the atmosphere and heal broken lives and emotions. The truth delivered in love becomes a healing force in a marriage relationship; the truth withheld, or spoken intemperately, becomes a weapon that devastates.

At the outset, let me make two important distinctions about "the truth." On the one hand, the truth as a proposition or principle has the power to become an anchor in our lives. Biblical or other self-evident universal truths reveal to us something about the nature of God and His creation. Most of us sense inherently what's right or wrong, and if we really don't know, we can easily discover the nature of the moral law by referring to the Old and New Testaments. I firmly believe that there are universal moral absolutes that we affirm or deny at our peril. These truths demand to be lived and obeyed regardless of whether or not we articulate them to one another.

For example, it's the truth that adultery in marriage is always wrong and fidelity is always right. You can accept these propositions or reject them. But your response doesn't make them any less true. Your reaction just determines the degree of spiritual power you will have in your marriage. If you reject the truth, you lose power; if you accept it, you gain power.

There is also a second form of truth, a more dynamic type, which involves an active proclamation of reality. This is truth that must not only be lived; it must also be conveyed through the spoken word. The reason is that this kind of truth is not always as obvious as the kind that can be stated in clear-cut moral propositions.

If your spouse has been treating you disrespectfully in social gatherings, for instance, you must give her the facts about how miserable she makes you feel when she does or says certain things. You must share the truth with her as you perceive it. After all, she may have unintentionally slipped into some bad habits and may not even be aware of their effect on you until you tell her. Only then, when the problem is clearly stated and placed on the table, can the two of you begin to explore the right way to relate to one another in the future. Such truth, which demands to be expressed openly in words, requires unconditional honesty between two people in an intimate relationship.

A tough marriage must be built upon a foundation of both these types of truth, the proposition and the proclamation. But it will surely be destroyed by deceit. You see, without truth, there can be no trust. Without trust, marriage is no more than cohabitation, a physical relationship without communication.

So if you find yourself in the midst of a serious conflict with your spouse, start looking around to see what exactly is true in the dispute and what is not. Once you identify the truth about your problem, take these steps: First, accept the truth yourself. Next, state the truth to your spouse. Finally, begin to act on it.

Once the truth has become the guiding principle in your marriage, you may find at first that the situation gets worse before it gets better. But believe me, that's just a temporary phase, as you are maturing as a couple. The words of Jesus "... the truth will make you free" (John 8:32) might easily be applied to describe the "after" state of your marriage once you've begun to proclaim that which is authentic.

The problem most of us face in marriage at one time or

another is that we become entangled in a webwork of misunderstanding, manipulation, and even lies. Yet the truth has the power to cut through these shackles and set us at liberty.

For example, you and your mate probably don't always see specific situations in quite the same way. Furthermore, you each may perceive the truth in a different way. That's why you have conflict; and that's also why you must *speak* the truth—to clarify the understanding each of you has about the situation. Open communication will also help you understand one another's feelings, hopes, and expectations. If love and respect have slipped away, speaking the truth will help you regain them.

Now, let me share with you a concrete example where I had to speak the truth first in order to get a couple to see it and begin to speak it themselves.

These two young people had only been married about two years. They came to me because their marriage was already on the rocks. They were actually ready to split, but they were confused about whether that was the right decision. One of the reasons they hesitated to go directly for a divorce was that they were both serious Christians who believed that divorce was wrong in most cases.

Well-meaning family members were already strongly encouraging divorce. "What's to be gained by staying together in an unhappy marriage?" one in-law argued. "There's more to life than sticking with a relationship that should never have happened in the first place."

But the couple accepted the authority of the Bible, and somehow they couldn't reconcile divorce in their situation with the teachings of Scripture. There is really only one reason given in the Bible for a divorce between two people who believe in Christ: marital infidelity.

As I became more familiar with this couple's background and with the fact that they both did, indeed, have a firm faith, I realized that only one solution would be right for them: They were going to have to try to stick together and work their problems out.

First of all, I felt that saving their marriage was the *right* thing to do. I felt it was the truth. Also, I knew that if they got a divorce, they would soon have to grapple with serious feelings of failure and guilt. That almost always happens after a marriage breaks up. What's more, there would be new conflicts, both personal and financial, for them to face as single individuals. Even more importantly, they would probably always wonder what would have happened if they had taken the Scriptures seriously.

So I stressed that it was God's perfect will for them to have a permanent marriage and that they should try to work things out. As we talked, I let them know how much I felt for them. I liked them both, and I sensed to some degree the hurts that were causing them both to suffer.

Also, I was aware that they were under a lot of pressure to call it quits. They were hearing strong statements of the "wisdom of the world" from their family members, friends, and probably plenty of other marriage counselors. And the main message they were getting on all sides was: split!

But I told them straightaway, "I feel for you both, but I have to tell you the truth: You don't have any biblical grounds to seek a divorce. So stick it out!"

In the course of subsequent meetings, we discussed the ways that God can give us power to work out problems that seem insurmountable. We explored principles of effective prayer and the true meaning of Christ's love, which He empowered us to show to others. Gradually, they came to grasp the possibility that they might be able to work things out and stay together. And, wonder of wonders, they could even see a glimmer of hope that they might fall in love again!

There was no "quick-fix" miracle in this case. Rather, it took very hard work and solid commitments for this couple to cement their relationship once again. But they did it, and today they actually have one of the strongest marriages I know about. In fact, they have started an informal lay ministry in their church to help other struggling couples get over potentially devastating marital hurdles.

The hero in this story, of course, is truth. The truth was proclaimed; the couple accepted it; and they began to work out their difficulties on the basis of what they knew to be right. They didn't know where they were going at first. In fact, I didn't even know where they were going. But since the track they were on was morally sound and true, I had every reason to be optimistic. They could be certain that their final destination, even though it was nowhere in sight when they first met me, would be exactly where they wanted to go as a couple.

One problem with my argument, however, is that telling the truth can be a harsh proposition. Suppose, for instance, that your spouse says romantically, "I know we agreed not to eat out any more this month so we can save some money, but I'd really love to try that new little French bistro across town. I hear the food is delicious. Why don't we make one little exception just this once, and then we can go back to the budget tomorrow?"

That's a siren song that could be the first step into financial hot water. But after all, your mate means well. She's probably just trying to introduce a little excitement into your relationship, and that's an admirable motive. So it really won't do to reply, "Get thee behind me, Satan!"

In dealing with such a situation, it's important, first of all, to recognize that there are no degrees of truthfulness. It may be hard to *discover* exactly what's true. But it's not the truth itself that's fuzzy or "gray." It's your perception of it.

Yet an understanding of this point doesn't solve your problem, does it? Even after you've identified the truth in a problem, there are different ways to speak that truth to your spouse. You can hit him over the head with it and perhaps shame and alienate him. That's the sort of approach that gives concrete meaning to the old adage "The truth hurts."

Or you can proclaim the truth with great sensitivity. You can often phrase the truth so that it invites the other to a thoughtful, honest response instead of a defensive response to an attack or accusation. That's what can come from speaking the truth *in love*. To understand this point better, let's examine four "love handles" that should help you grasp how best to express the truth effectively to your mate.

Love Handle #1: Use the language of love.
One careless word in the heat of the moment can destroy years of trust and intimacy. Saying impulsively, "I always thought you were stupid, but this takes the cake!" or "Let's face it, I didn't marry you for your looks!" can sound the death knell for a close matrimonial tie.

So it's important to be especially careful in those conversations when you're feeling unusually anxious or apprehensive. Verbal attacks will only add fuel to the flame of argument. The result could easily be an all-out verbal slug fest.

A common mistake is to put one's partner on the defensive by saying something like, "I'm mad at you. Now, what are you going to do about it?"

Such a comment reflects a self-centered attitude that shows little regard for the other person's views. Also, it paves the way for a defensive, retaliatory remark and an inevitable escalation of the verbal conflict.

Instead, you might say, "I'm feeling very upset about this situation, and I really don't want that to happen. Can you help me? Can we try to work this thing out together?"

That approach will help you avoid a judgmental or blame-placing tone and will also provide your spouse with an opportunity to participate in some solution. You might say this is the tough-marriage commentary on the old saying "You catch more flies with honey than vinegar."

It's also important to remember to avoid a harsh tone of voice and aggressive gestures if you hope to show that you truly want a resolution. In other words, try not to jut out your jaw, jab the air with a hostile finger pointing at your partner, or allow your voice to take on a strident, accusatory edge.

One of the most common problems I run into with couples

who have a communication problem is the failure to recognize the effect of aggressive body language and threatening voice tones. One wife told me that her husband consistently made her defensive and angry. We were able to isolate the exact circumstances and cause of her negative reaction. Her emotional thermometer began to rise when his voice assumed a didactic, "instructor's" tone and also when he used powerful hand movements to emphasize his points.

Interestingly, when she pointed out what he was doing, he said he was totally unaware that he was the one who was creating the problem. He saw that she was reacting negatively to him, but he couldn't figure out why *until she informed him.* As it happened, he was merely using decisive, attention-getting gestures and tones that he employed in business meetings in his office. There, the reaction was always measured and emotionless. But at home, other dynamics in the husband-wife relationship set the stage for frequent explosions.

So remember that your tone of voice and your body language are as much a part of the language of love as the words you use. When King Solomon said, "A soft answer turns away wrath, but a harsh word stirs up anger" (Proverbs 15:1), he must have had the marriage relationship in mind.

Love Handle #2:   Be patient.
A popular proverb, restated in various ways by Disraeli, Matthew Arnold, and others, says, "genius is patience." But perhaps the oldest authority for the value of this virtue is the apostle Paul, who lists patience as one of the all-important "fruits of the Spirit" (Galatians 5:22).

In any case, whatever the original source of wisdom, this quality of patience is absolutely essential to speaking the truth in love. You see, even as you and your spouse are becoming one in your marriage relationship, you have to deal with the fact that you're also two different people, with different backgrounds. You may be one, but you'll never be quite the same—and you shouldn't be. Part of your strength as a marital unit is the variety of wisdom and experience you can bring to bear when you face different challenges and problems.

You and your mate will often respond to the same situation in quite different ways. Some people require a great deal of space and time to reflect on decisions. Others are quick reactors who jump right in and make their best judgments.

One couple, in listing the things they couldn't agree on in their relationship, said that a major problem on weekends was deciding what to do. The wife always knew she wanted to see a certain movie or play or go to a certain restaurant. Her husband, on the other hand, liked to ruminate and savor each decision, partly as a reaction to the fact that he had to make fast decisions at work during the rest of the week. Part of the unwinding process for him on weekends was the luxury of enjoying making decisions slowly and casually.

As long as the wife made the social decisions, the difference in their styles was usually compatible. But when the decision was put to him or when he decided at the last minute that he didn't want to do what his wife had planned, tempers flared.

The key to such differences in style is patience. Sometimes, if you can just *name* the virtue you need, that's enough to get it. Try saying, "I have to be more patient with_____." Or if you believe in prayer, you might try praying for this quality as a fruit of the Spirit. But don't necessarily expect to acquire it overnight. I've known people who prayed for years for a specific virtue and it took plenty of, yes, *patience* to wait for its eventual arrival.

Also, sometimes it's best not to leap into trying to settle certain problems completely on the spot. I'm a great believer in *starting* right away on the resolution of a conflict, but not necessarily in reaching a final conclusion immediately. Impulsiveness in trying to eliminate a problem may be a deceptively dangerous strategy because it can lead to quick but superficial solutions. Getting to the root of some conflicts in a marriage may take weeks, months, or even years—especially if it took that long to create the problem in the first place.

So when you start to speak the truth in love, be prepared to hang in there for the long haul.

Love Handle #3: Look for important little ways to change your behavior around your spouse.

This third way to get a handle on speaking the truth in love to your spouse may at first blush seem to have little to do with language. But think about it for a moment.

When we carry on a conversation, it always occurs in some context. People react to us, or we react to them, in large part because of the relationship we've built up (or failed to build up). The most meaningful and constructive conversations are between those who are in the habit of showing respect and love for each other. And one of the most powerful ways we show respect and love is through our behavior—especially *little* acts and gestures that show we truly care.

I emphasize the word *little* because it really doesn't take much to touch off a major marital explosion. It's those little annoyances over long periods of time that build up and finally break the camel's back.

I constantly encounter couples who identify among their major problems such habits as a tendency on the part of the mate to interrupt in a conversation. The solution I often suggest in this particular situation is to develop a set of signals to let the offending partner know you're irritated. For example, the one being interrupted might just lower his head and raise his hand until the interrupter has stopped and offered an apology.

So it's the seemingly small, inconsequential actions, the minutiae of everyday life, that can threaten your marriage most seriously. Maybe you annoy your spouse with clothes littering, mud tracking, nail biting, or even eating crackers in bed.

If your spouse has complained about your actions, her concerns may seem trivial at first. But don't take her comments lightly. Thank her and tell her you plan to change your behavior starting now. Then, *stop it*, or at least pursue the offending behavior outside her presence! Sure you may slip every now and then. But if you make an effort, that at least shows your spouse you really care.

These, then, are some negative considerations, some offensive practices you might work to stop. But there's also a *positive* side to showing love through little gestures.

I know one husband and wife who have a very bright and frisky three-year-old son. They seemed the picture-book couple and it seemed that they should be completely happy, but they weren't. The problem was that the mother found herself going bananas and running late every morning as she tried to get the youngster dressed for nursery school. She began to resent the fact that it seemed entirely up to her to manage the boy each morning. Fortunately, however, before she had been completely pushed over the edge by circumstances, her husband noticed something was wrong.

"What can I do to help?" he asked.

"You can dress him," she said without any hesitation. That wasn't quite the response he had expected, but it was true, it was specific, and it was manageable. He was sensitive enough to realize he should respond immediately.

So the father rearranged his own early morning schedule to make himself available for his son and help get him dressed. As it happened, Dad could distract and entertain the child more easily than Mom at that time of day, so it took him about half the time to dress the youngster. In the meantime, the woman was able to get her own early morning chores out of the way at a more relaxed and efficient pace. The couple found they had eliminated one important pressure point that sometimes had interfered with the tranquility in their relationship.

What I'm talking about here is obviously not a complete

personality change. In some cases it's just a matter of making a few small but key moves to remove roadblocks or smooth the way to better communication. A few flowers, a book by a favorite author, or maybe even doing some shopping that your spouse would have to do—that's all it takes. The little gestures show in concrete ways that you really care. Speaking the truth after you've helped create a loving sort of an environment is often a relatively easy task because you've already said through your actions, "I love you."

Love Handle #4: Pray together.
Let me inject a personal note here. Whenever my wife, Jane, and I are frustrated or confused about some family problem or we're unsure about which direction to take, we always take it to a higher authority. Now, this may not be too easy for you. Even when both a husband and wife have a firm spiritual commitment, it's not always so easy to pray together. Many couples may feel uncomfortable or even embarrassed at first.

There are several possible reasons for this attitude. First of all, even if you consider yourself a religious person, you may not have had much experience in prayer. The best way to remedy these feelings of inadequacy is to plunge right in and learn something about it.

But there may also be another reason for your reluctance to pray. You see, when the two of you bow your heads before the Lord and ask Him to settle your dispute or give you mutual guidance, you are taking a risk. He may very well not respond in the way you want or expect.

A key principle for finding God's will in prayer is that you have to sweep aside your preconceptions and *listen* with an open mind. That can be disconcerting. In fact, when you first begin the adventure of prayer with your spouse, you may find the experience profoundly unsettling, as though you're just letting go of the side of a swimming pool in your first attempt to swim.

Even though we sometimes still experience this sense of

nerve-racking uncertainty, Jane and I have prayed together often enough that we know in general what the end result is likely to be. When we both submit ourselves without reservation in prayer, we *always* sense a kind of settling down, which reduces and often completely eliminates our anxieties.

The reason for this peaceful feeling is that genuine prayer makes us aware that God is at work, building bridges of reconciliation that are beyond our powers. We realize that we're not alone in dealing with our problems. In fact, as our prayer proceeds, we often find we really don't have the problem we feared. The weight of our cares and burdens has shifted from our shoulders to His.

This fourth and final way to get a handle on communicating directly but lovingly is really the master key to the entire process. After authentic prayer, it's almost impossible not to speak the truth in love. God Himself is the essence of truth; and He is also love. If Jane and I together are in touch with Him, that automatically makes all our communication problems easier.

I believe the same thing can be said for you as well. The old truth "let go and let God" applies here. When you pray together, you *let go* of your anger, resentment, and negative preconceptions. You also *let God* renew and reestablish His love in you and your love for one another.

So why not try it: Invite God to mediate in your marital conflicts and confusions. If you and your spouse seem to be talking past each other or *at* each other, turn the conversation into a three-way affair. Then you'll begin to talk *to* each other. And you'll also find God can introduce an amazing degree of understanding and compassion, even in those marriages that may have seemed hopeless.

THE FOURTH COMMANDMENT

Break Bread Together

Not long ago, I was meeting with an old friend to discuss some mutual business interests. While we lingered over coffee, enjoying a brief respite from busy professional schedules, our conversation turned to family matters.

Before long, I got the distinct impression John was struggling with some serious conflicts, though he coated his words with a steady stream of lighthearted banter. Finally, he came to the point of what was bothering him. Leaning closer to me, he whispered confidentially, "Have I ever told you about the vanishing dinner table at our house?"

He was still smiling, but I could also tell there was a genuine seriousness to what he was about to say. At first, I imagined an exotic, Poe-inspired table of paranormal activity or criminal intrigue. But he didn't relate any such story of horror or suspense. Instead, I heard the rather commonplace account of an American family who couldn't coordinate their schedules to manage a meal together! The result was the prospect of disaster for what had once been a solid, meaningful marriage.

The facts were relatively simple, and I've heard the same story, with slight personal variations, time and time again in my counseling sessions. John's children, in their teens, had multiple school and social commitments that frequently took them away from home at the dinner hour. John often had to work late to keep up with the demands of business. His wife, who had her own career opportunities outside the home, was also scrambling around with civic and church interests.

As a result, the microwave oven and automatic dishwasher worked overtime to keep up with the many eating shifts at the "family" dinner table. Meals had become a refueling operation rather than a communal gathering.

Even as my friend lamented the loss of his family time, I was amazed at how perceptive he had been to identify the lack of a common meal as central to his family's problem. Many times it takes an entire counseling session or more to get to the heart of the matter. But John had an advantage: He came from a long tradition of jovial family meals, and he missed the companionship more than most people.

After all, the dinner table is the one place in our homes where family members are most likely to come together for an intimate gathering on a regular basis. Regardless of how small or large the family unit may be or how improverished or magnificent the dwelling, almost every household has the potential to allow family members to "break bread together."

Too often, however, we allow the dinner table to be defined in other terms. It becomes primarily the place where we receive nourishment for the body so that we can hurriedly get on to more important things. But in fact, mealtime should be much more than that.

The dinner table is the traditional symbol and practical center of family togetherness. It's the place where we eat, talk, relax, and enjoy the company of those we love most. There, we are in a strong position to nurture the corporate body and soul of our families and marriages. At the table, we can communicate with each other most freely and lay the groundwork for tough husband-wife ties that can survive the strains of stressful relationships away from home.

Perhaps most important of all, coming together for a meal provides the opportunity for a profound experience of spiritual unity. Each partner in a marriage becomes preoccupied with his or her own concerns during most of the day. But when a couple and their children get together for a meal, they have the opportunity to focus more on each other and their joint family interests. It's easier in a dining room setting to clear the mind of individual distractions and concentrate on the other person.

On the other hand, the wrong approach to a family meal may shatter any possibility of family unity. If there is any underlying conflict or dissension when you gather together at the table, the discord may become even more intense and obvious simply because of your very physical closeness. But if you can find ways to keep the hostility and anger in check, the act of eating together can become a major gesture of reconciliation, a sort of olive branch that constitutes the first step toward greater harmony and peace.

So family tables are much more than utilitarian pieces of furniture. They provide the setting for expressions of warmth, love, and resolution of conflict. And it's not just the traditional evening family meal that has the power to enhance oneness in a marriage.

For example, many harmonious couples start off the day by giving each other a smile and kiss at the breakfast table and then sharing the first meal together. With this simple ritual, they set the tone for a more constructive relationship during the rest of the day. Words aren't really a key part of this experience. It's the warm touch and loving presence that make all the difference. A regular tradition of such breakfasts can transform an entire marriage as the couple gets used to enjoying each other quietly.

In a similar way, your budding relationship with your spouse was probably influenced greatly by meals you shared while you were dating. I'm sure you can recall hamburgers at the local drive-in, a pizza after the movies, or a picnic in the park. Also, there were probably memorable dinner dances, festive buffets, and that all-important first dinner with your prospective in-laws. Each of these meals became part of the wooing process and encouraged increasingly deeper sharing that led to some of the most meaningful conversations of your life. At those times, you learned to relate in new ways to that one special person in your life.

I can still recall the early days of my own marriage, when the kitchen table was a center of my daily relationship with my wife, Jane. We lived in a small apartment in Boston that was so limited in space that the eating surface literally became our headquarters. It served as study desk, typewriter stand, catch-all for family business papers and, most important of all, the place where we fed our bodies and our dreams.

Beyond these early memories, I'm sure you also find that there are other special meals that you associate with the high points in your family life. Relaxed dining during holidays, festive weddings, and milestones like christenings and bar mitzvahs—these are all celebrated, at least in part, around dining tables. Food enhances feelings of hospitality and personal connection. It's also a means of offering comfort to those in the valleys of life. Hence, we may prepare a meal for family or neighbors when there is an illness or death. A husband who normally may not serve as cook may voluntarily and lovingly take on the role of chef when his wife is bedridden. An offering of a meal can become a universal gesture of goodwill, a means of extending strength and hope to others in their time of need.

For me, the prototype for the most meaningful mealtime experiences is the Last Supper shared by Jesus and his disciples. The Bible tells us that the night before his death, Christ and his twelve closest followers gathered to celebrate the Jewish feast of the Passover. During the meal, Jesus took bread, blessed it, broke it, and then passed it around to his disciples to eat.

"Take, eat; this is my body," Jesus said.

Then he took the cup of wine and, after giving thanks, passed it also to the disciples: "Drink of it all of you; for this is my blood of the covenant, which is poured out for many for the forgiveness of sins" (see Matthew 26:26–28).

This "Communion" service has been replicated by Christians around the world ever since that night nearly two thousand years ago. Jesus gave us the ultimate illustration that food can mean more than mere nutrition. Indeed, he referred to himself as the "living bread," to show what an intimate relationship there is between what nurtures our bodies and what strengthens the spirit.

Still, it's important to remember that collective dining doesn't have to be limited to special occasions. The day-to-day routine of breaking bread during family meals is vital to the sustaining of our closest relationships. But how, specifically, should we relate to one another at mealtimes? Is there a special technique or style of dining that can enhance the experience and draw husbands, wives, and other family members closer together?

I've found that we can learn how to relate more meaningfully to our spouses and also our children by observing what I call an etiquette of life during family dining. Ordinary etiquette teaches you when to use the right fork and spoon and how to project a smooth, cultured image at a dinner party. But there's much more to the etiquette of life than mere table manners.

I've found that observing a few key principles of this special kind of etiquette can help transform a family mealtime into a deep sharing experience that will surely strengthen your marriage. Let's examine each in a little more detail.

Etiquette-of-Life Principle #1: *Every meal should begin with prayer.*

Saying grace before each meal helps us acknowledge that the act of eating involves sources of energy and blessings far greater than physical sustenance. Prayer reminds us that there is a higher authority at work in our lives and makes us more aware of our dependence on God for everything, including a healthy marriage.

Sometimes it's hard to maintain the discipline of common prayer, especially if some family members are in a hurry or if only the husband and wife are present. If you're not accustomed to praying spontaneously out loud, it may seem safer to ask a child to recite a memorized, rote prayer rather than do it yourself. Yet these opportunities for spouses to pray together in informal, close family settings can bind the couple together in ways they might never experience otherwise. To pray conversationally, one on one, with any other person will always transform the relationship.

Finally, the strongest marriages tend to be rooted in something beyond the humanity of the individual husband or wife. Prayer at mealtime, which usually begins in thanksgiving, recognizes our basic dependence on God for everything. If we choose to pray, we automatically assume that we are depending on God to oversee the expertise and safety of those human beings who help to put the food on our tables. We are giving thanks for the farmer, dairy worker, fruit picker, packager, trucker, grocer, and the hosts of others who lubricate the food chain. Behind all these mortal agencies, we acknowledge in a brief prayer of thanksgiving that we depend on God for rain, sunshine, and fertile soil to start off the whole process of food production.

A mealtime prayer, then, is a timely reminder of our totally dependent condition. Sometimes we can fool ourselves into believing we're completely in control of our lives. But that's when we—and our marriages—start getting into trouble. Grace before each meal helps us keep in mind that a higher force is always at work in all our daily relationships.

Etiquette-of-Life Principle #2: *Meals teach us the basics of servanthood.*
Every meal is a time of giving and receiving, serving and being served. In fact, the way you eat can indicate some sig-

nificant things about your basic character and how you will participate generally in social situations. Consideration at mealtime produces respect and sensitivity around the conference table, the assembly line, the office desk, and the retail counter.

In commenting on what it took to be great in the kingdom of God, Jesus said that the greatest person would have to become the least and the servant of all. Taken the wrong way, this teaching could be reduced to the simplistic notion that a person should become a doormat. In the profoundest sense, however, the words of Christ become a clarion call for sensitivity, consideration, and graciousness.

On one level, Jesus is saying to us as we sit at the dinner table, "Remember: Many factors have contributed to this meal. Someone has worked to pay for the food. Someone has shopped for the food. Someone has prepared it. Someone has cleaned up the dining area and set the table attractively. As the meal begins, someone will pass a dish to you, and you will pass it on to someone else. Everyone is serving and being served; it's the style with which you carry out your servanthood that makes any meal a success."

There is a trend in some homes for the children to eat separately from their parents, but I think this is a mistake. In fact, I like to see small children seated next to their parents or between older siblings. This way, they get an opportunity to observe and copy proper table manners. Also, they learn more effectively how to interact with people older than themselves. And if their elders are acting as good models, the youngsters will see how to become good servants, in the best sense of that word. As youngsters learn to give, receive, and express thanks at mealtime, they'll tend to carry over those habits in their daily dealings with others.

Of course it's up to the parents to set the tone for dinner table encounters with gracious eating and serving habits and a polite manner of speaking. A proper approach to conversation and etiquette at the dinner table usually will help anyone, children as well as adults, carry over qualities of sensitivity and considerateness to their other relationships.

One top executive I know uses mealtime conduct as an indicator for choosing employees for management positions. After he's sure that everything else about a person checks out, he invites the candidate to dinner. Then, throughout the meal, he observes how well the person initiates conversation, how thoughtful he is toward others, and how courteous he is at the table. This executive then makes his final judgment based in part on these impressions.

This discerning businessman believes any positive professional skills a job candidate may possess comprise only a part of the total picture. If the person is preoccupied with himself and insensitive to others at the dinner table, it's likely that this pattern will spill over to other situations. At least, that's the conclusion this executive has come to after years of observing those who work for him.

Conversely, if the candidate observes social courtesies, puts others at ease, and in general shows those all-important qualities of "servanthood" at the dinner table, that probably indicates he will be well received in the marketplace.

The lesson for you and your spouse is clear: Examine the way you relate to one another at mealtimes. If the atmosphere is strained and unpleasant, look more deeply into your entire relationship to see what may be going wrong. As you begin to correct the problem, resolve first to improve the way you treat one another at mealtime. If you try being a servant at the table, then you may well find that an entirely new element of warmth, understanding, and even romance has been introduced into your life.

Etiquette-of-Life Principle #3: *Breaking bread together can teach you patience in your marriage.*
Almost everything that's important and meaningful in a marriage takes time. So anything you can do to nurture this quality of patience will get you that much closer to a tough,

resilient relationship. Mealtime is one of the best times to
begin to forge this all-important virtue.

But I'm not saying it will be easy. When food is in the vi-
cinity, we have all sorts of forces working against us in our
quest for patience. We see the act of eating as merely a way to
satisfy hunger, not a means to build patience.

Babies learn very quickly that by crying when they're hungry, they're more likely to be fed. And usually they pop that
food into their mouths as soon as they can get their little
hands on it! As they grow older, kids learn they must somehow control the primeval urge toward impatience. But most
of us don't succeed completely in controlling our inner urges
and our appetite for immediate gratification. I know countless adults who get quite irritable if they have to wait even a
few minutes beyond their usual dinner time.

Because this deeply ingrained tendency toward impatience
is a powerful force, it's advisable for husbands and wives to
face their impatience squarely. They need to talk about their
cravings openly rather than let them fester. Unfortunately,
most of us would rather die than admit that we're feeling
testy simply because we need to stick some food into our
mouths. But if you can communicate with each other about
your need to improve on your own patience, it's much more
likely that your children will learn a little something about
this essential quality themselves.

I know one husband and wife who had a problem with impatience at mealtimes until they were finally able to overcome
embarrassment and anger and sit down to talk about the
matter.

For instance, they discovered there was often some time
when they were out of sync with each other as the last-minute
details of food preparation were being completed. The husband sometimes lingered a few extra minutes over the evening newspaper, thus allowing the food to get a little cold.
The wife, for her part, occasionally was late serving the meal
because her responsibilities at work caused her to get home
later than usual.

They also discovered during their meal-delay analysis that it was quite likely that one or more of their three children would get to the table after everyone else was already seated. Then there were the one- or two-minute delays that always occurred as extra dishes were placed on the table, preliminary conversations were wound up, and table grace was offered.

But despite these aggravating lags in starting the meal, this couple was able to overcome their problem. Just by recognizing that delays were likely to occur, the husband and wife were able to anticipate them and incorporate them into their expectations about when the meal would actually begin. It's always much easier to be patient about the forward movement of life if we know what to expect and how long it's likely to take us to get to the next benchmark in our lives.

Also, they found there were some practical steps they could take to make the delays more palatable. For example, if the husband was the one who was left cooling his heels because of his wife's lateness, she got into the habit of serving him immediately with an appetizer, such as a dish of fruit.

But beyond such nitty-gritty, stop-gap measures, this couple came to view the delays as an important slowing-down process. They found they were better able to make the transition from their breakneck daily existence to the more relaxed pace of dinnertime.

Perhaps the most significant benefit that accrued to this couple from their insights about patience at mealtime was the way their actual eating process slowed down. If you're impatient to return to some project when you sit down to eat, you're more likely to hurry through your meal.

Many times, this impatience may come out in gestures that can undermine the table's tranquility. Attacking your food like a vacuum cleaner, for instance, will only promote indigestion and overeating. But bolting a meal sends a message to your spouse and children that you don't really regard the time you're spending with them as all that important.

Only when both husband and wife learn and practice patience can they realize the full benefits of the meals they

share. Moreover, the attitudes they establish at the table will
be likely to spill over into other areas of their family life. The
entire atmosphere of the home can improve if only we introduce a little patience at dinnertime.

*Etiquette-of-Life Principle #4: Be creative in your ap-
proach to table talk.*
As we all know, there are people who have problems initiat-
ing conversations. They may be shy, or perhaps they've just
never learned the art of casual conversation. The family dinner table can provide an ideal opportunity to develop those
speaking skills, both for spouses and for children.

Sometimes, if one of the family members is especially
gifted in sparking stimulating conversations, it may be possible just to rely on him or her to get things started at each family meal. But in most cases, to get the talk going on a
stimulating level, I've found that it's helpful to plan some sort
of focused discussion in advance.

In our family, for example, the Sunday dinner after church
is the time for these focused discussions. We try to concentrate on some subject that is related to our faith, such as the
minister's sermon, our respective Sunday School lessons, or
friends with whom we may have had interesting encounters.
By tackling such serious topics, we open the way for deeper
sharing about those things in life that really matter to each of
us.

This tradition goes back another generation, to my wife's
mother and father, who encouraged solid biblical discussions
during the Sunday dinner. Jane still has a small box of cards
with Bible verses printed on them that her parents used to
stimulate dinner-table conversations. Each member of the
family would memorize a verse and then, during the meal,
everyone would discuss the meaning of the passage and tell
how they felt it related to their lives.

I've recommended this practice to husbands and wives
who tell me they have trouble talking to each other and to

other family members about the things in life that really count. One family I know has instituted a practice that they call "table topics" every Thursday night.

It goes like this: Each week, a different family member leads the discussion, and the leader gets to choose the topic. The eight-year-old son has been known to choose lizards, marbles, and maple syrup. His teenage sister once selected her favorite subject, telephones. In that suburban household, no one is late for dinner on Thursday night and no one leaves the table early.

Now, consider for a moment how much you can learn about your spouse and children through such mealtime conversations. Just by listening to them chat about topics that are close to their hearts, week after week, you *have* to get to know them better. There's no avoiding it.

Oh, there may be some stiffness or reluctance at first to really open up. But after a few sessions, the self-consciousness will disappear and some real revelations will begin to come out. In this regard, it's helpful to remember that third principle of etiquette—be patient!

So far, we've focused mostly on the positive aspects of the dinner table experience. But this discussion wouldn't be complete without a consideration of the other side of the coin— what I call the "intruders," which can destroy the family mealtime. I've identified five of these "bad guys" that interfere with our breaking bread together. I'm sure after you've thought about it, you can contribute even more.

Intruder #1: Newspapers, books, and television.
Unless you're alone, never read at the table! Banish reading materials and television so that *they* don't banish meaningful conversation and closeness from your marriage! Real interaction can't take place unless everyone participates. The propped-up newspaper or magazine, the blaring radio, and the shimmering TV picture communicate bad vibes to

others. They say: I want to close you off right now. Don't bother me. This stuff I'm watching is more important.

An exception to this rule, of course, is when a meal is planned around a special television program. But don't use the special nature of any program as an excuse to make television watching a regular habit. TV-oriented meals should be few and far between. And I'd also suggest that any time you have a special television session, a discussion of the show should always follow it.

Intruder #2: Punishment of children.
In my opinion, children shouldn't be disciplined at mealtime. Meals should be enjoyed in a relatively calm atmosphere, and it's impossible to stay peaceful and unaffected when a child is being punished.

Art Linkletter once said that he never punished any of his children at mealtime because the practice always ruined the conversation. That doesn't mean he didn't tell his kids to sit up straight, use their napkins properly, or teach them good table manners. And if they really acted up, they knew they would catch it later. But he did try to postpone serious discipline until the meal was over.

Intruder #3: Squabbling between husband and wife.
Arguing between adults should never take place at the table. This bickering creates a negative atmosphere, sets a bad example, and upsets the digestive system. And let's be fair: If you don't allow your children to argue at the table, why should they have to sit through your disputes?

So if you and your mate have some unresolved conflict going on when you sit down to eat, agree to a cease-fire. Declare a truce, at least until after dinner, so that there's no unpleasantness. You may even find that the truce will turn into a permanent peace treaty on the topic in question. Sometimes, when you stop arguing, it's hard to pick up again where you left off.

Intruder #4:   Telephone calls.
I've found that the easiest way to eliminate telephone intrusions is just to tell the caller, "We're in the middle of our dinner. May I return your call in about thirty minutes?"

Unless there's a real emergency, most people will respect your candor and be quite willing to wait. But just don't forget to return their call!

Intruder #5:   Bad table manners.
I'm all in favor of informality at the dinner table. A stiff approach to eating really turns me off. But truly sloppy table manners are another matter.

There's a sign in New York City that reads, "Littering is filthy and selfish—don't do it!" I always think of that when I see a sloppy eater. Piggish manners are offensive to others, even those who love us, and they should be corrected so that we can encourage the respect of our loved ones.

Consider how many hours you spend with your spouse at meals, hours that should be devoted to cultivating your marital relationship. Poor manners will only get in the way of this effort. They reflect a general disregard for others and ignorance of what's proper in public.

In many ways, the family table is the proving ground for the ability of the marriage relationship to endure. Meals are a day-in, day-out affair that call for an ongoing commitment to other family members. Dinnertime offers a series of little tests, such as patience, punctuality, and cordiality. Over time, how we measure up in the face of these tests can loom large in a marriage.

Clearly, there's more to breaking bread together than just eating. To be a good dinner partner *every* night requires a long-term view of a marriage that must be affirmed in little ways every single day. Breaking bread with your spouse under these circumstances can reinforce the consistency, success, and overall toughness and durability of any marriage.

THE FIFTH COMMANDMENT

Strengthen Your Spouse's Character

What is character?

The classic definition is that it's the entire "package" of attitudes, values, convictions, actions, and reactions that tells us something about a person's basic nature.

Good, solid development of our inner webwork of character traits helps us make the right moral and ethical decisions, even when everyone else seems to be on the wrong track. Character enables us to persevere in line with our fundamental principles, like some sort of modern-day Job, even when we are wounded by tragedy, failure, and rejection.

So what exactly does character development have to do with your marriage relationship?

The degree of strength of your character will determine how you make decisions, handle difficult challenges at home, and grow consistently from all your family experiences, both good and bad. In fact, character can mean the difference between compatibility and incompatibility in a marriage; it can make or break a relationship.

You see, many marriages fall apart because one partner continues to grow in character and the other does not. One couple in their late twenties who had this problem came into my office for counseling after the birth of their first child. As the young woman had settled into motherhood, her values and perspectives on life had changed. She keenly felt the responsibility of preparing her daughter for the world outside the home, so she set out to be the example she wanted her child to follow.

Among other things, she rejoined an active church and worked in the community for social and educational improvements she felt would eventually benefit her daughter. Also, she spent as much time as possible with the youngster in outings and activities designed to enhance the girl's character development.

In the process of helping her daughter grow into a good person, this young mother found that something exciting was happening inside herself as well. Her *own* character development had taken a sharp turn for the better. She found that her own religious faith had been rekindled and her values had become more family-oriented. The inner transformation, which gave her renewed strength and vitality, was remarkable to everyone who knew her—except her husband.

Unfortunately, this young man had refused to participate in his wife's new interests at home. He continued in the same patterns that the couple had established early in their marriage. Family outings with a toddler tagging along were not the thing for him. He gravitated instead toward childless pursuits—discos, bars, late-night snacks, adult movies, and other such entertainment. His wife had participated in those activities before their child was born. But now, they couldn't afford regular baby-sitters and had trouble finding one who could sit on a moment's notice when they did have the money. So she usually couldn't accompany him. Consequently, he spent many nights "out with the boys," retreated into television when he was at home, and grew more and more distant from his child and his wife.

In effect, the values of this husband and wife headed in different directions. Or it might be more accurate to say that hers developed and grew and his became stagnant and even began to decline.

That's an important point, by the way: Character can never stay the same. Either it gets stronger or it grows weaker. The combination of values and attitudes that make up character may *seem* to stay the same over a period of time. But actually, in this situation, character is ossifying and degenerating; it's becoming less and less capable of meeting new challenges and responding to unusual people and pressures.

But now back to the couple in question: As their values moved farther and farther apart, so did the original basis for their compatibility as husband and wife. They didn't like the same pastimes; they didn't enjoy the same people; they didn't dream the same dreams. Gradually, their relationship crumbled, despite my efforts to get them back on the track in our counseling session.

In short, this wasn't a success story. The marriage ended in divorce, mainly because this husband and wife had waited too long before they confronted the basic differences in their character development.

Perhaps by this point we all agree that character development is important in a marriage. But agreeing in principle is one thing and putting ideas into practice is another. So how can a husband and wife work to strengthen their basic personalities and inner selves?

Many people find it hard to develop character on their own. It's one of those things, like New Year's resolutions, that seem great at the time but fall by the wayside as the stresses and strains and ingrained habits of daily life prevail.

Of course, some people don't even start out with good intentions. They simply resist character development from the outset. They shun responsibility for themselves and for others and run from activities that might encourage them to stretch and strengthen their inner fiber. This sort of negative attitude is a protective device of sorts, which some hope will shield them from "growing pains." They want to eliminate risk that accompanies change in their lives.

Unfortunately, whether a person tries and fails to develop his own character or never tries at all, the result is about the same: Personal maturity becomes impossible; growth of personal relationships is stunted; and character development comes to a standstill. And so does the marriage.

What I'm ultimately getting at here is this: Character development is too difficult and too uncertain to leave it only to chance, or to expect one partner to provide the character for both. No one individual can do that. If you don't give your spouse a hand here, there's a great danger that whatever progress does occur will happen at an uneven and unsatisfying rate. And that will probably be disastrous. So it's essential, as our fifth commandment states, that you must *strengthen your spouse's character* at the same time you work to strengthen your own.

In other words, you have to reach out beyond yourself if you want this fifth commandment to become a reality in your marriage. You have to set specific *double* goals for your mutual character development. If possible, those goals should be set by the two of you together. In other words, it's best if you can agree explicitly on what you want to achieve.

If you can't agree, then try this: On a low-key, relaxed basis, begin to promote and pray for those character values you want to see in your spouse. To this end, you might reinforce positively the good things and keep your mouth shut about the bad. To put it another way, it's important to learn to "stir up one another to love and good works," as the Bible says in Hebrews 10:24.

Already I can hear the objections: "Isn't this a violation of my spouse's integrity? Doesn't he (or she) have the right to self-determination? Why not just be tolerant of our character differences?"

It *is* important to be tolerant of individual traits and to recognize different levels of character formation. Each spouse is an individual and will grow in special ways that the other can't and shouldn't try to imitate. But please remember: Our ultimate goal is *unity* in the marriage. That means you want your spouse to reach his or her full potential; but you also want to become "one flesh," a two-in-one entity. So it's imperative that your different patterns of character development be compatible if you hope to increase the strength and level of understanding in your relationship.

The *characteristics* of good character can't be presented as an exhaustive list because the human personality is so complex, with an infinite variety of needs. But still, from the experience and writings of some experts on good character, it's possible to talk in terms of a few specifics.

The apostle Paul, for example, was deeply concerned about character in his letter to the church in Galatia. Calling these key inner qualities the "fruits of the Spirit," he included love, joy, peace, patience, kindness, goodness, faithfulness, gentleness, and self-control (see Galatians 5:22–23). Now, at first reading, this list may appear rather abstract. But the lives of good, godly people over the centuries have fleshed out these character traits.

Paul himself, for example, felt the need to go into greater detail about the first quality—love—in his second letter to the church at Corinth. That Greek seaport city, with its hustle and bustle and problems of public and private morality, has often been compared with New York City in our own day. And apparently, as in New York, there was a great deal of dissension, competition, and pride in Corinth, even among those in the early church, who were supposed to be living together in some semblance of harmony.

So in one of the most famous passages he ever wrote, Paul launched into a detailed examination of how the Corinthians should be loving one another. To refer to this word, he used the Greek word *agape*, which means a noble, unconditional love that ultimately proceeds from God Himself. It's not some sort of fleeting, romantic love; nor is it limited to friendship, as noble as that may be. No, the kind of love Paul (and Jesus, for that matter) referred to was this incredibly deep, profound, powerful force that is rooted in one's relationship with God.

In describing this sort of *agape* love, Paul said it's patient and kind. It's never jealous or boastful; and it's not arrogant or rude. Those who have this kind of love don't insist on their own way: they don't get irritable or resentful, even when things aren't going their way. They rejoice only in the right, not in the wrong. Finally, this godly love "bears all things, believes all things, hopes all things, endures all things" (see 1 Corinthians 13).

Now, keeping some of these specific traits of good character in mind, let's explore some practical ways that you can begin to strengthen your spouse's inner being and fiber. There are three main character-building concepts that I urge every spouse to incorporate as part of his or her marriage.

Concept #1:   Give a priority to patience, kindness, and self-control as you help your spouse develop character.
One of the primary areas where a couple must exercise these three key qualities is in sexual relations. Sex is very often the first critical issue you confront in a relationship, no matter what your sexual experience has been before you tie the knot.

Your first sexual experience may have occurred before marriage, or it may have been on your wedding night. But whatever your age or situation, sex in marriage will probably be altogether different from what you had imagined. You see, once you marry and the day-to-day routine sets in, unexpected responsibilities and stressful situations take a toll on sexual relations.

For example, I'm counseling a couple who lived together for several years before marrying. The woman acted to hold the man in the relationship through sexual activity. Once married, however, she allowed her true feelings about sex to surface: In short, she doesn't like lovemaking. The husband is hurt and disappointed—and also feels rejected and inadequate. Furthermore, he's having a hard time controlling his drinking and tends to get involved in extramarital sexual activity. The marriage is in deep trouble, all because these spouses neglected to concentrate on building character.

So after the marriage ceremony, you or your spouse may not have as much time, energy or interest to devote to sexual intimacy as you had anticipated. There's a dangerous fantasy that once everything is "legal" and you're living together on what's supposed to be a permanent basis, sex will get better and better. But in fact, couples may not devote the time or energy to the physical side of marriage that they had anticipated. External conditions, such as shared living quarters with other family members or long or unusual working hours, may change the equation. Also, the very product of lovemaking, a beautiful child, can ironically be the most disruptive factor of all to enjoyment of sexual freedom and development of intimacy.

So it's necessary to be patient when the circumstances aren't conducive to tender, meaningful sex. It's also important to be kind—for example, not to get irritated with your mate when she prefers to wait for a more opportune time. And it's essential sometimes to exercise self-control: That is, if you've had to go for a while without sexual release, there may be a temptation to look outside your marriage for satisfaction.

But that sort of infidelity can be devastating to your own character development and also to your spouse's. A *permanent* commitment to another always presupposes a degree of self-control in your conduct, so that your mate can learn to trust and depend on you, even in difficult and trying circumstances. If by your actions you encourage suspicion and a lack of trust in your opposite number, his character development will suffer accordingly. He'll actually become suspicious, and strain and worry will replace any possibility for joy and peace.

All of this is related, of course, to the natural body rhythms of each spouse. On the surface, this may not seem like such a serious problem; but if you've been married for a while, you know it really can be a big difficulty. Different physical metabolisms can disrupt a relationship unless both partners are willing to make adjustments.

For instance, I've counseled a number of couples where one person was an early riser, who literally started the day with a song, and the other was a classic "slug-abed," to use Shakespeare's phrase. In one such case, the husband was an incredibly slow starter who could barely pull himself out of bed and get to work on time. His wife, on the other hand, was typically up an hour before he was and often couldn't wait to get off to her own job.

The problem intensified on Saturdays, when the wife had to put up with her husband's grumbling until noon. By that point, he usually had finally adjusted to the fact that he was really up for the day. She, however, was starting to run out of steam by lunchtime and often preferred to lie down for a short nap in the early afternoon. The husband, meanwhile, was steadily gathering steam and wanted to take the entire family out for vigorous outings on Saturday afternoons. Not only that; he was still going strong at midnight—despite the fact that his mate had already retired an hour or so before.

They found they were frequently at each other's throats but couldn't figure out why until we sat down and discussed how they felt at different times during a typical day. When it became apparent we were dealing with clear-cut cases of the early bird and the night owl, we had some basis to take corrective action.

One remedy that worked wonders for them was for each first to recognize that he had to be patient and kind to the other. Then, we planned their days so that they stayed out of each other's way during those times when one or the other was impossible to live with.

So the wife was pleasant to her husband after he had first

awakened, but generally she let him get revved up by himself. She recognized that he was going to be more irritable then than later, and she resolved to put up with the bad and anticipate the good that she knew was just around the corner. She didn't push him to do anything demanding in those early hours; in fact, she mostly avoided him.

The husband, for his part, agreed to take the kids on a special adventure in the early afternoons on Saturdays so that his wife could get a little shut-eye. Then, she usually arranged to meet the rest of the family later in the afternoon, when her energy level had risen.

Now, I don't for a moment want to suggest that this preliminary arrangement we worked out was the ideal. The goal was just to set things up so that the couple could get along reasonably well with each other. Deeper tolerance and understanding of one another—in short, mature character development—would come later.

Of course, sometimes the problem goes beyond a person's inner time clock and centers on basic goals and dreams about the future. I recently spent some time working with a young husband who had jeopardized his marriage because he was impatient about reaching his professional goals.

This young man, who had only been married a few years, was full of ambitious dreams about the day when he would find great wealth and social prestige. His own father had reached these high objectives, so the son had a ready role model to spur him on.

But the younger man's problem was that he wanted the same status and salary as his father without putting in the same amount of time and effort. In fact, he turned down offers for several fine positions with reputable firms because they didn't offer the "big bucks" and senior executive status he felt he deserved. In effect, this misguided young man just sat around waiting for fortune to find him, dreaming of big success rather than taking the little day-by-day concrete steps to make it happen.

Meanwhile, his home situation deteriorated. His young wife was forced to support her dreaming husband at several points, when he found himself without a job and was uninterested in taking a position that he felt was beneath him. Each became more and more disillusioned with work, marriage, and life in general. After a while, he realized that their marriage was falling apart, and that was the point when he came to me for help.

It became immediately apparent that this young man's problem was basically one of character development. He lacked the patience and other basic virtues that enable successful people to make a go of their jobs, marriages, and friendships. In practical terms, what he really needed was just to sit down and draw up an action plan for his life. And that's exactly what we did.

Our first step was to define his goals, both at work and in his family life. I always recommend that a couple should discuss together their ambitions, both personal and professional. Then they should establish a set of joint priorities. It's a good idea to write these goals down, so you can refer back to them in case you get off the track at a later date.

By taking this step, you'll first clarify in your own mind what your actual goals are. Also, you'll have a more definite idea about where you want your marriage to be heading. And if you draw up this plan together, both you and your spouse will know exactly what each expects from the relationship. Just talking through these basic goals about what kind of people you want to be and what you want to achieve in life can be a giant step in character development.

With this couple, the goal-setting exercise helped bring them closer together almost immediately. The husband began to take a more practical approach to the job market: He accepted the fact that success in his career was going to take some perseverance and time, and he found a job that could at least get him started. His big dreams were still there, but now they had been tempered by a recognition of the concrete steps he had to take to achieve them. His wife, in turn, was relieved to see him get off dead-center in his occupational search. It was much easier to deal with occasional frustrations from an actual job than constant frustration from no job at all.

Finally, even as you try to show more patience and self-control toward your spouse, it's essential not to forget the third quality in this character triumvirate—kindness. I firmly believe that the best way to stimulate the growth of patience and self-control in each partner in a marriage is to encourage an atmosphere of kindness in your dealings with one another.

Most people admire patience and self-control in others. But kindness is the quality held in highest esteem. Down deep, we all want to be kind to one another; and we especially want to have the *reputation* of kindness and magnanimity. Of course when push comes to shove, a person may allow ambition, sexual temptation, or any of a number of other factors to take a priority over kindness. But even though we may be fascinated by various naysayers and villains, I don't know anyone who really wants to be a Scrooge or a Jack the Ripper or a J. R. Ewing. There's something inhuman about a person who completely lacks the "milk of human kindness."

Kindness, in short, is the lubricant that smooths the development of many other good character traits. I can still recall one young woman who seemed totally lacking in patience, self-control, and many other virtues. Yet she was a kind person; she meant well, and she had the reputation for possessing a "good heart." That is a solid foundation to begin to rebuild any marriage, because you almost always want to be around a kind person, no matter what other personality flaws she may have. Kindness breeds kindness and understanding.

Concept #2:   Get rid of the negative language and attitudes in your marriage.
Another important foundation for character development in a marriage is positive thinking. This is a principle of success

in life you may have heard so much that you feel it's too obvious to be considered seriously. But in fact, there are subtle ways that negativism can slip into our lives and begin to erode a relationship even before we're aware of what's happening. The most influential sages throughout every tradition and era of history have based much of their thinking on the positive and have criticized such negative traits as:

- dwelling on the failures and mistakes that you or others have experienced;
- boastfulness and arrogance;
- jealousy;
- too much "constructive criticism";
- demanding your own way rather than what's good for others as well;
- destructive backbiting and gossip;
- irritability and grumpy conduct;
- finding pleasure in another's misfortune.

Now, I realize that some of these traits may not normally be associated with negative thinking. But that's just the point: I'm convinced that most people think more negatively than positively about the big issues of life without even being aware of the trap they've fallen into. Now, let's go a little deeper into some of the above attitudes so you can see better what I'm talking about.

Jealousy and arrogance are especially destructive to character development because they can be detrimental to a person's self-esteem. For example, these days when a husband and wife may both be working in high-powered professional jobs, competition can crop up in a marriage. If the husband gets a promotion and his wife doesn't, that can lead to unhealthy comparisons. Or if the wife begins making more than her spouse, he may well begin to feel threatened, especially if he was brought up to see the male as the main breadwinner.

So it's very important to share your success with your spouse rather than gloat over it. That is, try to see the success experienced by one as the success of both. If one receives a larger salary, immediately begin thinking how the extra money can help the two of you *together* to lead a more fruitful and meaningful life. The one who does have the success should downplay it; the other should do the celebrating.

Above all, if you're not the one who got the promotion or raise, just remember: If you stick with it, your day to shine will come as well. When that happens, you'll be the one receiving the accolades—and in a position that will call for you to be humble and modest.

This principle doesn't apply just to money matters. I recall one situation where one of the children seemed to be more loving toward the husband than toward the wife. Unfortunately, the husband was somewhat insensitive. He became prideful about the special attention he was receiving, and that made his wife feel left out. I suspect she was also a little jealous, though she wouldn't admit this. We had a case of not so subtle one-upmanship at work here and that injected a destructive, negative element into the husband-wife relationship.

One thing that got the emotions in this marriage functioning properly again was for both husband and wife to recognize it was inevitable for their child to go through a series of developmental stages. These stages often involved relationships with the parents where first the husband and then the wife would be the favorite. There was nothing to be prideful or arrogant about. The child was just "going through a phase."

Also, in this case we analyzed how much time each parent was spending with the child in question. It turned out that the mother was devoting much less time to the child than she was to the other kids or to her job. The father, in contrast, was spending more time with his "favorite" than with the other children. So it was natural that the family relationships would have developed as they did.

After a considerable amount of discussion and soul searching, this man and woman finally recognized that first they had to adjust the approach that each of them was taking to their kids. They had to become more evenhanded in the amount of time and affection they devoted to each youngster.

But even more importantly, once they had made this adjustment, they had to refuse to allow any child's moods and preferences to dictate their own attitudes toward one another. Although the allegedly favored child was certainly an important part of the family, the *foundation* of any family's stability rests on the degree of love and oneness experienced by the husband and wife. When this couple finally began to see the situation for what it was—a subtle case of creeping negativism in their family relationships—they were in a position to strike off in a more positive direction.

Another kind of subtle negativism surfaces when you offer an ongoing stream of "constructive criticism" about your spouse's habits and personality. I can't count the number of times I've encountered husbands or wives who pepper their marital conversations with such observations as: "Dear, aren't you putting on a little extra weight? Who on earth did your hair? You really ought to talk less at dinner parties!"

One of the real zingers that can provoke anger or depression is to say, "You really did a good job making that presentation to the club members, *but* next time it might be a good idea not to . . ." It's that qualifying clause tagged on the end of a compliment that can really take the wind out of anyone's sails.

We're all guilty of this sort of negative talk. For some reason, our culture seems to encourage it. Allowing these habits to continue unabated could ring the death knell for a solid relationship. So I'd suggest that you do an evaluation soon of your own casual conversations with your spouse and begin to weed out the "constructive criticisms."

In fact, I know couples who have resolved for a period of a day, then several days, and then as long as a week, to say nothing but positive things to one another. You might think that would be impossible. After all, it's *necessary*, isn't it, to bring up some negative things, just to keep personal interactions realistic?

Actually, it's not necessary: Try it, and you'll see what I mean. Totally positive communications can come like a fresh breeze of renewal into a tired, downtrodden marriage.

Another sneaky negative trait that creeps into many marriages is irritability. Chances are that the real reason for your bad mood isn't even within shouting distance. But your spouse becomes an easy, available mark for any stress you may be feeling.

Unfortunately, the undeserved sharp retort and periodic edginess that stem from outside frustrations can destroy warm feelings in your home. One wife I know could always tell when her husband had run into problems with a difficult boss because he usually took out his pent-up hostility on her when he got home in the evening.

One night, for example, their children were acting up just before dinner, fighting over some toy that both wanted to play with. After about a minute of this argument, the husband blew up to his wife: "Can't you keep these kids in line? If you can't handle the discipline in this house, then I'll take charge of it—and then you'd better all look out!"

Both the wife and the children stopped abruptly, stunned at the outburst. The wife knew that the actions of the children didn't justify such a response. And my later conversations with this couple did indeed reveal that in this instance the husband had actually been fuming about criticism he had received from his supervisor at work.

It's important to talk such situations through and try to understand them; that was the first step toward putting this stormy marriage back on the right track. But some damage had already been done. Harsh words really *hurt* your spouse and children. The tongue is such a devastating weapon that a couple of words or sentences uttered in haste can cause wounds that last for weeks, months, or longer.

In a moment of strong emotion, one of the most powerful

negative weapons is to bring up old mistakes, fights, and other negative memories. "What can I expect from you—after all, you've already cheated on me once!" said one wife, referring to an extramarital affair her husband had engaged in years before. "How can I ever trust you again?"

Another devastating verbal thrust is to make disparaging remarks about a spouse's family background: "You're just like your father—cranky, overbearing, and slightly unkempt!"

My advice about this sort of behavior is to follow the old Hebrew prophet Jeremiah, who quoted the Lord as saying, "I will forgive their iniquity, and I will remember their sin no more" (Jeremiah 31:34).

Forgive and forget. Those are such easy words to say and so hard to do. Yet it's absolutely necessary, if you hope to build a strong, tough marriage, to forgive your spouse for mistakes and wrongdoing and *also* to avoid bringing up the old negative emotional "garbage" later. Unconditional forgiveness is really what true positive thinking is all about. You have to reach the point where you can really overlook past wrongs and focus primarily on what's right about your marriage. Then the door is open to dramatic gains in character development.

Concept #3:   Character development depends on a permanent commitment to the other person.

When you made the definite commitment to get married, you embark on the ultimate endurance test for a love relationship. In essence, you're promising to be there through thick and thin, come hail or high water. You're saying you're going to "tough it out" no matter what comes your way.

There has to be real backbone to a relationship to enable you to get through troubled times. As a matter of fact, it's the most difficult challenges that may cause you to grow more than when the sailing is smooth—but *only* if you're prepared. And the best way to get prepared is for each spouse to be in the ongoing process of strengthening the other's character. Build up your spouse, and you'll also be building up yourself *and* the relationship. Fail to support your spouse, and it's likely that the relationship will falter and perhaps fail.

Real love isn't merely a euphoric feeling. Feelings ebb and flow. The biblical principles for marriage stress loving your spouse as a child of God. When you do that successfully, your mate will most likely respond in kind and you'll both experience inner growth. Real love emerges from an inner foundation of trusting, caring, and sharing other-directed values. In short, real love is rooted in character development.

During my work over the years in premarital counseling, I've developed a checklist of seven questions that I ask prospective husbands and wives. Not unexpectedly, I've found that these questions also work for married couples who want to test the health of their marriage as they go along. The answers point up where the strengths and weaknesses lie in the relationship, and they are also a good indicator of where character building is needed.

You and your spouse may want to answer the questions individually in writing and then compare responses. Or it might be more beneficial for you to bounce the queries back and forth in a conversation. Either way, the answers can be used to work out many difficulties you may have in your relationship.

But here's one word of caution: Bear in mind that this is an exercise to build understanding—not a weapon to injure one another's feelings. If you do it together, keep the positive in mind: Look for areas where both of your characters can be strengthened. Remember, our goal here is to build those inner foundations, not destroy them.

Checklist for Character Building

1. *How would you describe yourself in general terms as a person?*
This is the basic question I use to find out what each person knows about his own character and personality. I'm in-

terested in finding out what one spouse is willing to disclose about the "real me" in front of the other.

A less mature individual usually has trouble describing himself in meaningful terms. For example, some people I've talked to may answer with a physical description and a list of hobbies: "I'm twenty-four years old, blond, have blue eyes, and I'm about ten pounds overweight."

Others may identify most closely with their careers: "I'm an engineer." This tells where their sense of self-esteem lies. But what happens to the *person* and the inner character if the job is lost?

Still others may give trendy or esoteric answers like, "I'm a very loving person." Or, "My goal in life is world peace." Of course, we all want world peace. But such abstractions won't help your mate or potential mate understand who you really are.

I've discovered over the years that the most mature answers—those that bode well for a marriage relationship—are those that show that the person values his work, and other activities and emotions, but that he can put them in perspective with his personal relationships. Also, the people with the strongest character are realistic about their physical attributes, and they have come to comfortable terms with their family and personal background.

I also look for an openness and accepting attitude in the answers to this self-description. A person who tends to be somewhat flexible on things is the type who can allow another to be "grafted" into his life on every level. There's usually a certain sense of inner security in such a person—an abundance of integrity, resourcefulness, and moral fiber. And there's also usually room for growth.

2. Where will you be in ten years?
This question is designed to help the couple understand and verbalize what they expect from the relationship on a long-term basis. Each needs to know the goals and ambitions of

the other if they hope to reach any meaningful level of happiness and satisfaction in their relationship.

Of course, many of the answers may miss the mark. Some people answer this question with a geographic location, like, "I'm hoping to live in California in ten years." Others see goals strictly in terms of occupational achievement: "I want to be at least a vice-president in my company by then."

But alas, even though many know generally what they want from their jobs, I've discovered that few have any realistic idea what they want from their marriage! There are a couple of common reasons for this: Either the person has no personal value system that has the power to affect and guide the relationship, or the individual is unaware that it's important to discuss and establish long-range objectives to use as a benchmark for success and progress.

So regardless of how long you've been married, it's a good idea to ask your spouse, "Where will we be in ten years?" or, "Where would you *like* to be?" The answer can help you identify exactly where you are personally in your own character development and can also move your relationship toward more meaningful goals. And if you consider the question together, you'll be more likely to make decisions about the future together.

3. What is (will be) your main problem in marriage?
There are hundreds of answers I've heard to this one! For example: "The economy . . . his salary . . . her parents . . . my temper . . . his ex-wife." You name it, I've heard it.

But even with the variety of answers, there are certain groupings that cause me more concern than others. When someone sees the problem as being rooted in his spouse, for instance, that bothers me. Often, such a response says, "You're the *entire* problem, not me," and it may reflect an unwillingness or inability to admit one's own faults.

It's also helpful to see how your spouse or "intended" will relate to what you see as the main problem. Sometimes, the reaction puts the main problem on the table for the first time in a relationship. Simply verbalizing it can become the major step to a solution.

For example, one wife, shortly after the birth of the couple's first child, said to her husband, "My problem is that I don't seem to love you as much as I used to. A lot of the spark has gone out of our relationship."

That depressed the husband, and he also felt a wave of anger sweep over him. After all, his wife was telling him that he no longer turned her on! But then in a cooler moment, he realized he was at least glad that he knew there was a problem, and he decided to do something about it.

He actually began to woo his wife again: He started taking her out more often. Also, he began stressing the positive in their conversations, such as telling her the ways he thought she was wonderful and avoiding those "conditional compliments" and "constructive criticisms" we talked about previously. He even brought her flowers and other small gifts every now and then.

The result? The romance came back into their relationship—all because they had considered openly, "What is the main problem in our marriage?"

Finally, I also encourage couples to ask themselves, "What will be our main problem in five years?" Under "non-combat" conditions, when you're just at the beginning of a potential problem, you can often avoid future difficulties. A measure of prevention can show you those weak areas that haven't yet caused a crisis and can give you the basis for a plan to build character strength into your matrimonial partnership for the future.

4. How do (will) you manage family finances?

When I ask this question in my counseling, I'm not trying to pry into anyone's personal pocketbook affairs. But I do regard the answer as vital for any marriage relationship. There are so many pitfalls relating to money matters that any misconception can lead to disaster.

For example, a major disagreement on priorities for family

income may mean that one spouse wants to spend a lot of money on entertainment while the other wants to contribute to a savings account. I've seen such a difference of opinion lead to frustration, arguments, and even divorce.

Also, I've run into a number of couples who don't share information about budgets and spending habits. Many times, the wife doesn't know where the money is going for such things as investments and insurance. Or the husband may not know how much is going into food or child-related expenses.

The operative word here is *partners.* Some people are by nature spendthrifts; others are stingy. Most fall somewhere in between. But in most cases, the husband's attitudes about money will differ sufficiently from the wife's that the stage is set for conflict—unless they sit down and answer this financial-goals question together.

This is an important part of character development, by the way. On the nitty-gritty level of family finances, we have to decide to "put our money where our values are." Some couples spend all their money on their own pleasures and vacations. Others put most of their money into their children. Still others bend over backward to contribute to charities and their church. Where you spend your money says something about who you really are, down deep. And if you can just find time to plan more sensitively and intelligently where you *should* be spending your money, you'll find you and your spouse reflecting more seriously on those inner values we've defined as personal character.

The practical solution to family financial problems is to sit down together and draw up a family budget. I've done this numerous times with couples who have come in to see me, and I've found it's the safest, most productive way to handle money matters. With a mutually agreed upon budget, you can see where your funds are invested and where they are wasted. Also, you'll both be more aware of how your disposable income is being used. Most important of all, if you work together to set practical money goals and plans for your marriage, you'll develop a sense that the money is "ours," not "mine" or "yours." And the result will be big dividends in character development in your marriage.

5. How do (will) you handle children?

Many people don't talk about this one until after marriage because they don't feel it's important until child-rearing begins. But some preparation, planning, and discussion well in advance will ensure a more pleasant transition to parent-hood.

It's fashionable—or practical, as the case may be—to post-pone having children. Many people want to get a little more money in the bank; or some wives may hope to achieve a cer-tain career status before they have to take maternity leave. So for whatever reason, starting a family when you're in your late twenties or even in your thirties has become much more common.

But no matter when the youngster arrives, big changes are going to occur in the marriage and great pressures are going to have to be confronted and managed. If you don't already have children, you might for a moment imagine relating to a baby twenty-four hours a day—after spending years only with your spouse. How will you deal with a cranky toddler in the middle of a restaurant? How much time will it take to oversee your child's education? Will you return to work immediately, or will you go back at all? Is the husband willing to take time off to be a "house husband," or at least to share the burden of child care?

Obviously, there are many possibilities that a couple can choose, and there's something to be said for a number of the options. But the key factor is that you should ask yourself this question and then reach some agreement as a couple about the approach you should take. Even if you already have kids, you may never have sat down to discuss your respective phi-losophies of child rearing. There's no better time than the present!

6. *How do (will) you handle conflict?*
Because conflict, including everything from mild disagreements to out-and-out verbal battles, is inevitable in marriage,
it's important to know in advance how you and your spouse
will deal with it.

Are you both willing to recognize warning signals and handle the matter promptly? Are you willing to help one another
resolve personal and mutual conflicts? How can you prevent
conflict? Do you already have areas of conflict—and if so,
what are you doing about them?

All of these questions should be answered openly and honestly as soon as possible, whether you're just thinking about
getting married or you're well into a relationship. In my opinion, conflict provides a key arena to test character development in a marriage. If you can get through a fight and feel
you've both learned something—and you both still love one
another—you're making big progress in strengthening your
inner value systems.

7. *What do you personally want out of your marriage?*
The question has been placed last, in part because it's an acid
test of honesty. Almost everyone has some specific self-interest to be served by being married. The ability to get some of
these selfish motives on the table can go a long way toward
helping spouses understand each other.

Of course, many husbands and wives will try to sidestep
this point. Some will say, "I don't want anything from marriage." But that's patently false. If you don't want anything,
why bother?

Other sidestepping answers are more subtle: I love my
spouse and just want to make her happy. . . . Marriage is the
natural thing for two people who love each other. . . . I'm a
traditionalist who just prefers making it legal.

All these responses may be quite true, as far as they go. But
there's always more, much more, that lurks beneath the surface. For example, I know we're beginning to get to the heart

of the matter when a spouse says, "I don't want to be lonely in my later years." Or, "Her family has a lot of money, and my mom always said, 'It's as easy to fall in love with a rich girl as with a poor one!' "

Certainly at first, most people who wrestle with this final question have a rather fuzzy idea about what they want from marriage. But if you think hard about it, you'll realize that there are some bedrock reasons that have moved you toward marriage. If you can muster the courage to discuss these motivations honestly with your spouse, you'll be much more likely to understand one another *and* get your heart's desire out of the relationship.

Above all, just keep this in mind: Your spouse can't read your mind! Unless you *say* something, you may spend most of your life waiting for some form of marital satisfaction that never comes. Of course, even when you tell your spouse what you expect from the marriage, you should do it with the understanding that she may not fully comprehend your concern. If you tend to be lonely and insecure and she's more independent, it probably won't immediately register on her that you actually got married to find regular support and companionship. After all, she doesn't particularly need that.

But just talking about your expectations is an important first step in drawing closer together and understanding one another more completely. By being open with one another on this issue, you'll see respective strengths and weaknesses more clearly. And you'll be in a much better position to help your spouse shore up inner weaknesses.

As I said earlier, character development is a matter of growth. If you want to help your spouse grow with you toward a better mutual relationship, that will require spending time together in a meaningful pursuit of inner strengths and values. And as both of you grow in character as individuals, there will be an even firmer foundation for oneness in your relationship as a couple.

THE SIXTH COMMANDMENT

Make a Commitment to a Community of Faith

Take a quick quiz:

NAME TEN MARRIED COUPLES YOU KNOW WHO WORSHIP TOGETHER ON A REGULAR BASIS.

Did you pass that one without consulting your annual Christmas card list for additional names? If so, you're probably already a member of a religious community.

Now, for part two:

ARE YOU AND YOUR SPOUSE ELIGIBLE FOR THAT LIST?

I know what you're thinking: what does our church attendance have to do with a book on marriage? My answer: Everything!

I believe, without a shadow of doubt, that your marriage will be strengthened by a mutual commitment to an active congregation. In fact, I'm willing to stake my reputation that if you and your spouse begin to participate *actively* in worship services and related religious activities, your marriage will be transformed.

Of course, there's a lot to be said about that word *actively.* Professional pollsters report that a large segment of the American public—consistently around 95 percent, according to a Gallup poll—believes in God. Another 40–45 percent attend church regularly, according to Gallup. And the interest in religion seems on the upswing: Two-thirds of the adults interviewed by Gallup in one recent survey said they were more reliant on God today than five years ago.

Apparently, though, the high interest in religion doesn't automatically translate into stronger marriages. Even as religious concern remains high, so does the divorce rate. Why should this be?

In my opinion, there are two big problems with the religion-marriage connection.

First of all, even if a person says he believes in God, that doesn't mean that he is truly mature in a spiritual sense. So it may be quite true that 95 percent of adult Americans believe there's a God, but how many go beyond that bare belief? For example, how many get involved in regular spiritual exercises, such as prayer, Scripture reading, and service work?

In fact, there are strong indications that many Americans, though they have some sort of basic religious orientation, are rather lukewarm in their beliefs and practices. National polls show that even though many people believe in God, far fewer read the Bible daily, engage in helpful activities for others, or meet regularly in prayer-and-share groups.

Also, just look around at the people you know: How many verge on being really *radical* in their spiritual commitments? That is, do they give God and their perception of His plan for them a top priority in their lives?

If your experience has been the same as mine, you don't run into too many of these highly committed individuals. In my own counseling work, I encounter many more people who see their religion as just one part of life (and often, a small part). As far as their marriages are concerned, they don't see their faith playing much of a role. Even if they think it *should* play a role, they don't know how to go about applying spiritual principles in a marital relationship.

The second big problem is that even if one or both partners have a deep spiritual commitment, they may have failed to take the all-important step of merging their separate commitments into *one*. As with our earlier discussion of unity or oneness in marriage, this doesn't mean that either partner must lose his individual identity. Rather, both spouses should just start tailoring and adjusting their respective spiritual commitments so that they mesh together in their daily lives as a spiritual entity.

In practical terms, this means first of all that a husband and wife should worship *together*. It's not enough to go to separate churches. Nor is it sufficient for one to attend church or synagogue regularly and the other to go to the same place sporadically. In short, spouses must worship together both at church or synagogue *and* in the home. In this way, they will be in a position to develop spiritually at a comparable pace; they'll be working arm-in-arm toward the same spiritual goals at the institution of their choice; and they'll relate jointly to a broader spiritual support community.

This last point is extremely important because no one—and that also means no couple who hopes to *become* one—can operate effectively in a vacuum. The traditional nuclear family, consisting of father, mother, and children standing alone and isolated as they face the world, is a *myth*. No family can remain self-contained and self-sufficient. We're all meant to be part of larger groups, and especially of a community of faith. So if a husband and wife hope to have a successful relationship, they must learn to fit their marriage into a broader network of spiritual relationships.

Worshiping together, then, is more than just a time-honored tradition. On a broader plane, the family practice of spirituality places God at the helm of all our important relationships. Both spouses and children become impressed with the fact that there is a higher authority at work in their daily lives. What better place than a house of worship to learn to "do unto others as you would have them do unto you"? And what better forum to apply such a principle than a family and marriage?

But now, in practical terms, how do you go about finding an appropriate community of faith? Also, when you've found a house of worship, how do you organize your life so that you make the most of it?

I'd suggest the following six steps. They've worked for me, for those I've counseled and taught, and for many others I know.

Step #1:   Establish some sacred time in your marriage.
In the Judeo-Christian tradition, we honor the example that God set when He rested on the seventh day, the Sabbath, after creating the universe, the earth, and its inhabitants in six days. But what exactly is behind this idea of taking some special, sacred time off?

One translation of Genesis 2:2, where it refers to God resting, is "God caught His breath." I like that image. If God needed time to catch His breath, surely we need it even more!

The Sabbath was set aside by God as a time for a change of pace, a time to recoup, a time to refresh the spirit. But people through the ages, right up to our own day, have found it hard to follow God's example. We get so involved in our daily activities, such as making money, playing sports, pursuing hobbies, whatever, that we think we just don't have time to stop for a while and take a breather.

I suppose God knew we'd have trouble disciplining ourselves to establish some sacred time to spend with Him and to build up our relationships with others. So he gave us a direct order, which He stated several times in the Bible: "Six days shall work be done; but the seventh day is the Sabbath of rest, a holy convocation. You shall do no work therein. It is the Sabbath of the Lord in all your dwellings" (Leviticus 23:3).

As you can see, my sixth commandment for a tough marriage isn't very original. As a matter of fact, it goes right back to the original Ten Commandments—commandment number four, to be exact: "Remember the sabbath day to keep it holy" (Exodus 20:8).

But the Sabbath wasn't just earmarked for a break from business as usual. That day stood for many things: worship, service, rest, and sharing. It was a time for communion and fellowship, not only with God, but also with others.

The classic observance of the Sabbath has been to devote a full day once a week to this kind of "time off." I don't know about you, but by the seventh day, after a week full of distractions, pressures, and obligations, that's just what the "doctor orders" for me. It's a regular time to reflect on life's meaning.

The commandment to keep the Sabbath holy is also a reminder to us married couples that we need time off. We need a change of pace, an opportunity to consider the purpose of life together. In honoring the Sabbath, we give ourselves permission not to bake, jog, shop, watch the stockmarket, or commute. God tells us to let the marriage *be* the marriage.

Dr. Norman Vincent Peale sees it the same way. In *A Guide to Confident Living,* he told of a doctor who prescribed going to church "at least once a Sunday" for his patients who suffered from fear, inferiority, tension, and related problems. Remarkable cures of the mind and spirit, as well as the body, have resulted in just attending religious services!

Peale's conclusion goes like this: "There are certain deep universal appeals to human interest and to these human nature always responds. There is no force equal to religion in its power to touch and to satisfy basic needs." I would also add that if you and your spouse make a joint commitment to observe this practice of one sacred day a week, you'll *immediately* begin to experience a strengthening of the ties that bind you together.

But even as I advocate taking one full day a week off to nurture your spiritual side, I don't want to limit this concept of sacred time. It's very important, as we'll see later, to set aside one day for joint family worship at an outside house of worship. But at the same time you can and should establish some special, spiritually focused moments on other days of the week.

Specifically, I'd suggest that you arrange some time for a family devotional. This is a traditional, time-tested practice that will take some effort and thought at first, but it will also pay off incredible personal dividends in your marriage. Here are some tips I've found to be helpful for starting an effective family devotional:

Set up a regular time and place for your devotions. You can't operate here on a hit-or-miss, ad hoc fashion. If you wait for the mood to strike you, you'll probably never even get started. Also, be sure to avoid all distractions, such as television or hi fi systems. I'd also pull the plug on the phone; it's too hard to tell some callers that you simply can't talk to them at the moment.

Family devotionals do take some planning, encouragement, and hard work, especially at first. But then, when you begin to realize the benefits, you'll be afraid not to have them!

Set the tone with a Bible reading. I don't mean that you have to have a full-blown Bible study. In fact, I'd advise that most families avoid a lengthy, formal study. It's really too hard to hold everyone's attention if you have a variety of ages and levels of spiritual development in your family.

But having offered these words of caution, I do want to say this: I believe it's essential to make the Scriptures your main source of authority when a question arises about the nature of God and the practical ways we should conduct our daily lives. And there's no better way to recognize this authority than by reading a short Bible passage.

Also, starting off with a Bible reading will put you into a listening mode. In this way, family members are more inclined to take in spiritual advice and principles than always try to dispense them.

Allow plenty of time for individual participation. As you,

your spouse, and perhaps your children get involved in these
devotionals, be sure that one doesn't dominate the discussion. After you've read from the Bible and perhaps from a devotional book, encourage each person to share his views on
what the passage or idea presented means *personally*. It's only
when everybody feels comfortable presenting private view-
points that the deepest kind of sharing and understanding can
occur.

✓ There's a related problem I've noticed in working with
many couples: the issue of the "spiritual leader" of the family. Inevitably, one spouse will know the Bible better than the
other or will have had more experience in church, worship, or
the practice of prayer. But if one of you seems to be a real
spiritual heavyweight, that can be quite intimidating to the
other partner.

I know one young couple, without any children, who decided it would be a good idea to begin regular family devotionals. They wanted to lay the groundwork for developing
spiritual depth and intimate sharing experiences in the future.
But the approach the wife used was so demeaning and devastating to the husband that they ended up in worse shape after
they had started the supposed "sharing" than they had been
in before.

For example, whenever the husband would hesitantly offer
some observations on a verse of the Bible, the wife would say
something like this: "Yes, years ago I used to think the passage meant that, but it's wrong. What Paul was actually saying was this. . . ." And she'd go on to expound on some
interpretation she had heard in a Sunday School class.

After a series of such putdowns, the husband stopped contributing his ideas. Then he started getting angry. And pre-
dictably, he began to find that he just didn't have the time to
continue with these devotionals. After all, who wants to sit in
a supposed "sharing" session where your thoughts don't carry
any weight?

When this young wife realized what she had been doing,
she was absolutely mortified! She had been completely un-

aware of how rigid, inflexible and insensitive she had been. And she quickly apologized.

"I know I can toss around a lot of significant-sounding religious jargon," she told her husband. "That's just my church background. But at the same time, I know I have a lot to learn about living a godly life—and about what all the religious jargon actually means. I can learn from you, so why don't we try those devotionals just one more time, and I'll do the listening!"

So even if one person is supposed to be the "sage" or the most advanced spiritually, the other should be given plenty of time for expression. The same principle applies if your kids are present. Let them have their say. Spiritual truths that have been "worked over" in the context of a supportive group are more likely to become a part of a person's life, and not just some abstract, intellectual concept.

Pray out loud together. Praying out loud together is one of the most difficult challenges that confronts many couples. I'm sometimes amazed at the number of regular church-going families I know who don't do this, yet there are some good reasons.

First of all, stating your concerns openly before God and your loved ones puts you on the line. It makes you vulnerable. Suppose you pray, "Lord, I know I've got a bad temper, and I'd like you to help me with it . . ." Or, "I know I didn't treat [your spouse] very well yesterday, and I want you to forgive me." That takes some extra openness, if not courage.

Secondly, if you're not used to spontaneous, conversational prayer, you may feel self-conscious. Many times in church, prayers can harden into a fixed form, a predictable part of the liturgy. They may come more from the head than from the heart. But spontaneous conversational prayers in a small group, such as a family, are *pure heart.*

Thirdly, even if you're experienced in this sort of devotional prayer, you may be reluctant to do it because you know the pressure will be on you to change.

One man I know who had fallen into the habit of belittling and bullying his wife in conversations knew he was doing wrong. We uncovered the problem and discussed it openly in some depth. But he couldn't take the next step. He just couldn't bring himself to pray, "God, help me treat my spouse better." Why? He knew if he uttered those words, the pressure would be overwhelming for him to immediately go out and start loving, rather than abusing, her.

But finally this fellow screwed up the courage to get the words out during a private prayer time with his wife. And sure enough, his prayers made him so self-conscious about his poor treatment of her that his pattern of behavior changed almost instantaneously.

So open family prayer imposes an imperative on the one praying to cause him, whenever possible, to become an instrument for the answer to his own prayer. In other words, if you're praying for the healing of a loved one somewhere far away, where you can exercise no personal control, you may have to rely on some agency of God other than yourself to help. But if it's within your power to help the situation, then God may very well begin to motivate you during prayer to go into action.

These, then, are a few ways that you can begin to set aside some "sacred time" in your relationship with your spouse. But they are just the beginning. The spiritual discipline that starts in your family will lead naturally to a broader community expression of your faith—one that will reinforce your emotional and spiritual ties with your spouse. And the first step into this broader arena involves finding a place to worship outside your family.

Step #2: Find a sacred place for worship in a spiritual community outside your home.
It's certainly true that the place where you worship God inside your home is sacred. And as I've said, it should be chosen carefully, so that the husband, wife, and children can relate on a deeper level, free of distractions and interruptions.

But it's also important to find an *outside* place of worship, such as a church or synagogue, where you can establish connections as a couple and family with a larger spiritual community. I've heard many people say, "I can worship God anywhere, anytime." That may be true. But we also all need the discipline and instruction that are available in a broader religious community.

There's nothing new about this notion, of course. In Psalm 122:1, King David said, "I was glad when they said unto me, 'Let us go into the house of the Lord.' " David, you'll notice, was really *glad* about the prospect of going to a community house of worship. He looked forward to spiritual renewal, kindred fellowship, and the opportunity to focus in a special way on his relationship with the Lord. In short, he had a well-developed conviction about the importance of the "sacred place" in his life.

For many people in ancient Israel, going to the temple wasn't exactly like a short drive to a local church. For example, those outside Jerusalem, where the temple was located, had to embark on a pilgrimage that might require them to be gone from home for days or even weeks. But it was well worth the effort, because of the spiritual renewal they experienced and also because they knew they were being obedient to God's command to worship together.

In more recent years in the United States, we've continued this tradition of regular group worship, though with our own particular set of Sabbath rituals. Consider the practice of putting on your "Sunday go-to-meeting clothes." Of course, there is a contrary trend, especially in some youthful urban churches, for parishioners to come to church in casual attire, including blue jeans and sports shirts. In part this is a legacy of the "Jesus Movement" of the late 1960s and early 1970s; and in part, it's a reflection of the more generally laid back attitude our culture has assumed in the past decade or so.

But getting out the best dress or suit is still part of the preparation many people—probably a solid majority of Americans—make once a week for a special spiritual occasion. This act is rich in symbolism, too. That is, just as we try to "dress up" our bodies, we also prepare our minds and spirits to be more receptive and reverent. In this way, we tend to be more open to spiritual renewal.

I've also always been impressed by the symbolic significance of the Saturday night bath in American social history. Why not a Monday night or Wednesday night bath? For most church-going Americans, it was a rite of preparation for the Sabbath—a cleansing of the body that would be completed the next morning with a cleansing of the spirit.

This impulse toward a corporate worship experience still moves us powerfully today. Down deep inside, we all *need* to reach out and make connections with a spiritual group. On the one hand, we're individuals who need to have a one-on-one encounter with God; but we're also communal creatures who need meaningful human relationships. When we enter a house of worship or any other community of faith, we are saying, "I'm not some sort of island. I was created for fellowship with others. In fact, my *spouse* and I were created for fellowship with others."

But of course entering a house of worship means much more than just making human connections. Our relationship with others becomes truly meaningful only as we all relate to God. In the act of worship, we all place our troubles, our gratitude, our entire beings, in the hands of the highest authority. The sacred place is not our turf but God's.

So be careful as you look for a house of worship. Husband and wife should shop *together* for a church or synagogue with the vigor of consumer advocates. The community of faith you select should meet the individual needs of each member of your family and also the special needs of your marriage. Also, there must be an *authority* there that you won't find anywhere else. So be sure that the guidance provided for you and your family comes not from human wisdom, but rather from a powerful proclamation based on Scripture and a belief in the living God.

Step #3:   Begin to build sacred relationships.
Once you've chosen a house of worship, it's easy to become a
mere "pew warmer." That's a person who gets there just as
the service starts, leaves right after it ends, and doesn't make
much effort to go beyond a minimum level of involvement.
Unfortunately, a huge number of Americans seem to fit into
this category. As a result, their chosen house of worship has
little impact on their personal lives or on their marriages.

If you want to go beyond this passive stage—and you *must*
go beyond it if you hope to receive any real benefits for your
marriage from your chosen community of faith—the first step
is to reach out to form new relationships. The most logical,
and potentially the most important, is a member of the
clergy.

God's main representative for you may be a priest, a rabbi,
a minister, or even a lay person. But whoever this leader is, he
should be able to foster, nurture, guide, teach, and inspire
you and your spouse to plumb the deeper levels of faith. Also,
the key clergy person in your life is there to remind you that
you are not your own keeper. The success of your marriage
isn't just up to you and your spouse. In the final analysis, like
it or not, we must all answer to a higher authority.

The most obvious way that husband and wife strengthen
their relationship is by participating together in the regular
weekly service. The spiritual leader will guide you through a
period of praise, prayer, Scripture reading, confession of
wrongdoing, and forgiveness. I advise married couples to listen well during every phase of the liturgy, singing, and sermon. God has something for you somewhere in there: It may
be hidden in some unlikely creed you've been saying all your
life. Or perhaps His word is embedded in a sermon that
seems otherwise boring or uninspired. But believe me, it's
there—and your marriage will come out tougher and healthier if you'll just keep your ears open for the message.

Beyond the regular service, the clergy person is there to do
pastoral counseling and to give other individual guidance.

But don't think he or she is the only one capable of handling such responsibilities. If you're in the right kind of community of faith, there should be a number of lay people who can give you spiritual support as well.

One young woman I counseled came to me after her husband had walked out on her. He had suddenly decided that family responsibilities were not his ball game, so he just bowed out of the picture. So there she was, left to pick up the pieces of her life and start all over again, with full responsibility for supporting herself and her two small children. The stress was tremendous, and as she told me, sometimes she felt like "short-circuiting." That's when I suggested that she join a caring church.

She responded to the idea, and after a few months in her new congregation, this young woman discovered she didn't need me any longer! Not only did she find emotional and spiritual support at her church, but the members also reached out to help her in other areas.

First of all, they offered reliable baby-sitting contacts, and some church members even volunteered to watch her children when she couldn't find a sitter. She also joined a prayer-and-share group. There, several other women listened compassionately to her personal problems, prayed with her, and helped her to come to important decisions about how to deal with her estranged husband. This group became an essential part in this young woman's life because she had found no one else that she could talk to, no one who really seemed to care.

This woman also got involved in some church outreach programs, such as helping feed the hungry in her neighborhood. That gave her additional purpose in life and also got her mind off her own problems.

Moreover, she was surprised to find that when she got into a financial bind, the church stood ready to provide some concrete aid. When her new church friends learned of her financial struggles, they gave this woman and her children food, clothing, and money—without compromising her dignity.

They made it clear that their help was a gesture of caring, not a handout. And she, in turn, saw their aid as a debt that she would repay later, by passing on the favor to others who were less fortunate when she got on her feet.

What this woman's experience boiled down to was a classic example of a religious extended family, a support system that she could never have found anywhere else. It was a modern-day commentary on the words of Christ in Matthew 25:40: "Verily I say unto you, Inasmuch as ye have done it unto one of the least of these my brethren, ye have done it unto me."

In this case, when a marriage had already broken up, the church stepped in to help one of the spouses pull her life back together. In other instances, where both spouses are already members of a congregation, I've seen the support community act in time to *save* a marriage. If both the husband and wife are solidly "plugged in" to an outside family of faith, then it's much more likely that concerned church members will take the initiative, contact the estranged parties, and help them patch things up.

But even as I exude enthusiasm for this supportive function of worship centers, I want to be realistic. As we all know, no community of faith is perfect. Some are so lukewarm or even cold in their spiritual commitment that they are incapable of providing the kind of support system that a married couple needs. Others may have the basic ability to help you out, but periodically you'll find they fall short. There's no individual or group in any church that will always live up to your expectations of what a Christian is supposed to be.

But you have to expect problems and shortcomings when human beings are involved. After all, as someone has said, the church is not so much a haven for saints as a "hospital for sinners." We need the church because of our inadequacies. And because we are human, there will occasionally be rifts and disappointments, even in the most promising community of faith. On balance, however—*if* you choose wisely—you'll find that a worshiping community can do wonders for your marriage.

Step # 4:   Enroll in a "spiritual school."

As we've seen, a community of faith should offer an opportunity for a married couple to worship together as well as chances to build supportive, outside relationships. But there's more. Relationships in themselves aren't enough to provide the entire foundation for a worshiping community. There also has to be a solid underpinning of knowledge and information—and that's what religious education programs should be about.

The amount we don't know about God and His will for our marriages always far exceeds what we do know. So the more we can learn about biblical principles and how to apply them in relationships, the more successful and meaningful those relationships will become.

There are many ways to increase your background and knowledge of spiritual principles. These include Bible studies at your place of worship; seminars on the spiritual dimensions of the marriage relationship; weekend retreats that focus on marriage enrichment or more general spiritual subjects.

This is another point to consider when you're choosing a church or synagogue: If they offer solid courses in the Bible, theology, and practical ways to express faith, that's a major plus. And I'm talking about *solid* teaching programs, not trendy offerings you could find in a local Y or social club.

In short, in my opinion your community of faith should have a clear-cut point of view that is based on the Scriptures. And that viewpoint should be taught in practical terms. In other words, you don't want an overwhelming dose of abstract theology, which you can't understand well enough to apply. But at the same time, you certainly don't want a lot of fashionable pap that may seem "relevant" to current affairs but doesn't offer you any reliable, authoritative guidance.

That's one reason I recommend a biblical emphasis. The Bible provides the best, time-tested ground upon which a marriage can flower. And after all, a major reason you want to get involved in a church or synagogue is to be able to put down the firmest possible roots to shore up your most important earthly relationship.

You take special pains for a ten thousand-mile tune-up on your automobile, don't you? So this week, take time for a "marriage tune-up" at your house of worship. If you find an adult education class and begin to participate in the discussions and study programs, you can *expect* great things to happen! At the very least, you'll increase the chances for a long and happy relationship that will run as smoothly as any well-tended car engine.

Step #5: Seek out opportunities for joint service.

So far, most of what we've said about the faith community deals with taking in help or getting nurturance for the marriage. But there's another set of possibilities that might be even more important. That's finding an opportunity to turn your attention from yourself and your marriage to the needs of others. One of the best ways to achieve this is through *joint service*, where both husband and wife, and sometimes the entire family, work in tandem to help outsiders.

Here's what I'm talking about. One family I know in New York City sensed that even though husband, wife, and children were going to church regularly, they lacked an overall sense of family purpose and camaraderie in their spiritual lives. In fact, they tended to do almost everything in life separately, and as a result, the family members were growing farther and farther apart.

But the husband and wife were wise enough to see that something was wrong. After a couple of serious discussions, they came up with a strategy to bring everyone together again and at the same time to put down deeper roots into their chosen community of faith. They had seen a few other families get closer as they worked on some single specific mission. So they decided they would try the same thing.

Because they all had a deep sense of compassion and of the need for social justice, the most logical kind of project to pull them together was something related to helping the poor. As it happened, their church sponsored a lunch program for poor people who couldn't afford to buy regular, nutritious meals. So this family made a joint decision to pitch in and help out—*together*.

Now, every Saturday morning they arrive in time to help make sandwiches, serve the needy, and clean up. Everybody is there—husband, wife, son, and daughter—for a total of about three hours each Saturday. And the results in promoting marital and family unity have been marked.

First of all, the project has served as a "team spirit" builder. For this limited period once a week, it's "all for one and one for all"—a real old-fashioned family enterprise. The satisfaction of knowing that at least one task has been confronted and accomplished successfully together carries over to other family gatherings and activities.

Secondly, nobody is the clear-cut "general" in the project. Each person has to participate vigorously and really "get his hands dirty." That generates greater respect and a sense of cohesiveness that comes from knowing that you've rolled up your sleeves and worked down there in the trenches with a real comrade-in-arms.

And believe me, the job that this family has taken on isn't all that easy. Most of the patrons of this church soup kitchen are less than fastidious in their personal hygiene. Also, there are plenty of alcoholics and drug users who drift in, looking for a handout.

At first the children, who had had little to do with people outside their own middle-class friends, were somewhat disconcerted. But they learned how to relate to these people, in part by watching their parents' example and in part by jumping into the job and getting the feel of the situation through direct contact.

Interestingly, since they've been participating in this project, all the family members look forward more to their own family meals. Why? Because many times their conversation turns to feeding the hungry, a subject in which they are all deeply involved and have growing expertise. Sometimes they consider how the lunch program could be changed for the better or how they could relate more effectively to the needy men and women they encounter each week. In the process, they share insights about the poor with each other in a way that helps them see beneath the filth and poverty. Perhaps most important of all, they're learning to replace pity with compassion. Also, they are continually reminded of how thankful they are for the blessings of their own home.

And this is just one example. I know another couple, without children, who decided to take the concept of a joint service commitment one step further. They designated *every* annual summer vacation for a large-scale mission project. In effect, each year they become volunteer missionaries for their religious denomination by participating together in some outreach program in Mexico, Central America, or a poverty-stricken area of the United States.

Instead of spending their vacation money on luxury hotels and first-class travel, they may work with poor Latin Americans in a medical facility or do evangelistic work with the overseas arm of another ministry. But they don't in any way consider their vacations a sacrifice. The people they meet and the places and situations they encounter are far more exciting than bus tours and four-star restaurants. They see exotic sights through the eyes of the inhabitants of these lands, and they form lasting friendships with individuals they would never otherwise meet.

Most important of all, this husband and wife grow closer together as they plan each summer adventure: "Who will we work with this year? What will we learn? Who will we be able to help?"

Such team efforts always help foster closer family ties. In fact, actually working together on some project close to the hearts of both husband and wife is probably essential to the deepest experience of marital oneness. It's only through the regular sharing of spiritual experiences that a complete kind of unity can emerge.

Step #6: *Share financial blessings with your family of faith.* This final step in embracing a communal spirituality is no substitute for giving your time and effort to the community. But it's just as essential for those husbands and wives who hope to participate fully in a church or synagogue.

Churches are always looking for extra money because they do need operating funds. But that's not all there is to it. There are some other dimensions of family giving that are very important for you personally.

First of all, making a commitment to give a significant amount of your family income to your worship center requires, once again, a joint decision by husband and wife. If you're going to do it right, you both have to sit down, discuss your spiritual goals, and decide you're going to put your money where your values are. That can be an exciting and unifying kind of experience.

Also, by deciding to contribute your money to God's work, you're affirming in a concrete way that your marriage is linked, body and soul, to that broader family of faith. You're not just giving lip service and you're not just limiting your involvement to your time. You're saying that God has control over your money as well.

How much should you give?

The traditional amount established in the Old Testament is a tithe, or 10 percent of your income (e.g., see Malachi 3:10). That may seem like a lot of money, especially if you are accustomed to contributing the average 3 percent of income that most Americans give to charity. Actually, the New Testament standard is even more rigorous than the tithe—both Jesus and Paul advocated *sacrificial* giving, which may amount to even more than 10 percent (see Luke 12:33; Luke 21:1-4; 2 Corinthians 8-9).

But why should you even consider such an approach to

giving? After all, isn't it true that financial problems are a major cause of marital discord? And won't you be exacerbating conflicts over money if you and your spouse start trying to tithe?

At this point, rational arguments in favor of the tithe don't go too far. From a down to earth, dollars-and-cents viewpoint, it doesn't seem to make sense to give that much money away. Often I've heard money managers and financial counselors tell people, "You simply can't afford to tithe!" And it's quite true that as I help a family draw up a budget and we search for an acceptable bottom line figure, it's sometimes hard to see where the tithe is going to come from.

Still, when a couple has been willing to step out on faith and make a commitment to give 10 percent of their income to God's work, the money always seems to appear from somewhere. What happens, I believe, is that a universal spiritual principle begins to work—a principle that we can't understand in terms of ordinary accounting procedures. In short, when we begin in faith to give significant amounts of money to God, He responds by making that much money, and oftentimes *more*, available to us in return.

Jesus stated the working of this principle rather well in Luke 6:38: "If you give, you will get! Your gifts will return to you in full and overflowing measure, pressed down, shaken together to make room for more, and running over. Whatever measure you use to give—large or small—will be used to measure what is given back to you" (Living Bible).

What a promise! And I'm here to tell you it really works!

For example, recently I began to work with one couple who were the parents of two small children. The husband had lost his job when his factory had laid off hundreds of workers.

But this couple was better prepared than most for this seeming disaster. You see, before this husband became unemployed, he had brought in a good income and both he and his wife had been extremely generous in sharing their monetary blessings with others. They had given more than a tithe to their church, and on top of that, they had helped a number of other individuals and families get over some hard times. Now, however, the tables were turned. The husband wasn't trained for other work, and he couldn't seem to find another job, no matter how hard he tried. The wife was agonizing over whether to hire a full-time baby-sitter so that she could go out and supplement the family income. To make matters worse, creditors were beginning to breathe down their necks, and the mortgage on their home was even in jeopardy.

It was at that point that the principle articulated by Christ came into play. First of all, their past generosity hadn't gone unnoticed. Many of those whom they had helped out of financial jams began to respond with small gifts of money. Also, others in their church community who had come to respect them and their commitment to God's work began to give food and clothing, as well as money. Within a couple of weeks, they had enough to pay their mortgage and buy the basic necessities of life for at least a couple of months.

Then other unexpected blessings began to pour in. Extra cash came from an unanticipated tax refund and also a small bequest from a relative who had just died. Now they had enough to make it for at least six months. Finally, the word had gone out in the church community that the husband needed a new job. After a couple of possibilities had fallen through, a position paying almost as much as his former job opened up.

Now the circle of giving and receiving was complete. Of course, this couple hadn't originally given in order to get. In other words, they hadn't contributed money with the idea that it would be returned to them in some way in the future. Rather, they had given simply because they knew God wanted them to and also because they experienced tremendous excitement and satisfaction in sharing their material blessings. Yet even as they gave, they triggered a spiritual process that eventually redounded to their benefit when they needed help.

* * *

So as you can see, there are many ways that a married couple can become meaningfully engaged in a community of faith. And I believe that at a minimum, a husband and wife should be in the process of taking each of the six steps we've outlined above.

But even as you participate more fully in your church or synagogue, keep this in mind: *Both spouses must get involved together!* If either of you makes a unilateral decision about your church, that will reduce the chance that you'll both be equally involved and that your marriage will derive the full benefit from involvement. Also, if one of you gets too far ahead of the other in the level of your involvement, that can be detrimental.

One may have to take the lead in pursuing outside religious activities. But if you happen to be blazing the trails, don't let yourself get so far ahead of your partner that you lose sight of him. The community of faith adventure must always be a joint experience. Otherwise, God's ability to support your marriage through the spiritual input of others may wax and wane.

THE SEVENTH COMMANDMENT

Get Rid of the Lust in Your Life

There's a word game we used to play with our children on long car trips to help break the monotony, and I wouldn't be surprised if you've played it too. We called it word association, and it goes like this:

I might say, "Italian," and then you say the first word that comes into your mind—such as "pizza."

I say, "winter"—you say, "Palm Beach."

I say, "lust"—and you say, . . . "sex."

Well, maybe you don't; but many people do see a direct and inseparable link between lust and sex. And more than that, they may see lust as something of a positive factor. If you've got good sex in your marriage, the thinking goes, then you just have to have a good dose of old-fashioned lust. In short, many couples accept lust as a natural and inevitable part of their lives. As a result, they fail to recognize it for what it really is—a destructive force that can undermine healthy marital sex and then go on to destroy the very foundations of the matrimonial relationship.

148

The association between lust and sex is understandable in our society, I suppose. In fact, lust and sex sometimes almost seem synonymous. Lust automatically comes to mind when we talk matter-of-factly about one-night-stand sex, group sex, casual sex, extramarital sex, and drunk-as-a-skunk I'm-sorry-I-did-it sex.

But lust—especially the kind of lust you need to guard against in your marriage—goes far beyond sex. As a matter of fact, lust is *any* excessive desire, any uncontrollable urge for immediate gratification. Although sex is an obvious target for lust, it's only one among countless others. The main motivation behind lust is to feel better *fast*. And that means capturing the object of your lust. Once you've got your prey in hand, that's supposed to relieve you of the gnawing desire, to satisfy that desperate need that says, If I don't have it, if I can't do it, my life will fall apart!

Lust may involve a craving for food, alcohol, sports, new fashions, job promotions, or many other things. The only common condition to unleash lust is that you must want something and believe you've got to have it right *now*. The pleasure won't be deferred for later fulfillment. And if you find you just can't get what you want, you may get so frustrated that you lose your ability to think and reason clearly.

We're all victims of lust to some degree. I know the sweetest little old lady who thinks she can't live without chocolate candy, even though she's diabetic. She's usually either unhappy or under medical treatment.

Then there's a doctor friend who absolutely has to indulge in chess several evenings a week, even though his passion leaves his wife alone and frustrated. I even believe there can be a lust for electronic temptations like television. A career woman I know locks her office door every day, no matter what other pressing matters are on her desk, so that she can see her noontime soap opera on a miniature TV she keeps in a drawer.

Now, some of these little lustful compulsions may seem more like harmless quirks than vices. But lust of any type is dangerous because it's self-centered, mechanistic, inflexible, and insensitive to the needs of others.

Take the seeming innocuous needs of the rabid football fan. A relaxing afternoon of NFL action is certainly something I can appreciate. But did you ever see a die-hard football addict at a wedding reception during the "game of the century"? It would be comical if it weren't so pathetic.

I recall one situation where a husband was chomping at the bit to get back to the television during such a reception. He was restless and came just short of being rude to new people he met. His wife was obviously getting embarrassed and a little irritated, and I could see that they were only one step away from some harsh words. Sure enough, he exploded at her, and before long, they were both headed out the door—I suppose to pick up the last few minutes of the game.

In this case, both spouses had to pay a high price. The wife had interfered with her husband's lusting relationship with his football team—but it turned out to be a lust that just couldn't be denied. "It was *your* cousin's wedding," I heard him growl as we walked out the door. "It was *your* idea to go. It was *your* fault I missed the game."

Clearly, he couldn't control himself unless he satisfied his lust *now*. And his wife had become the fall guy for this lust. She was playing second fiddle to this craving he had, and to some extent their relationship had started to wobble under the pressure.

Of course, a situation like this could continue to careen further out of control. I've known other marriages where the husband's lust to see every ball game has prompted him to take money earmarked for a new refrigerator and buy a new video cassette recorder. He wasn't about to miss any big game if he had to be out of the house! The wife and kids took a definite back seat to football during the season, as this man's lust caused him to confuse fantasy with reality.

The consequences of lust are bound to affect any marriage relationship because the emphasis is on what *I* want rather than on what she wants or on what's best for both of us. As a result, lust, which is nothing more than a drive toward selfish gratification, usually interferes with true intimacy. That is, it undercuts the emotional and spiritual bonds that must be present if you expect a physical relationship to have staying power or even to improve, like a fine wine, with age.

So clearly, it's important to get rid of the lust in your life if you hope to build a strong marriage. But the first and most difficult step may be just identifying what is lust and what isn't. For example, even though sex is often associated with lust, not all intense sexual desire is automatically lustful. I've known plenty of married couples who could hardly wait to climb into bed together and who carried on passionate sex lives—but without being lustful at all.

How can this be?

This brings us back again to our basic definition of what lust really is. A wildly satisfying sex life may be completely devoid of lust so long as each partner gives priority to the other's pleasure and enjoyment. But when one spouse begins to focus primarily on his or her own private pleasure, the stage is set for lust to bound upon the scene.

Lust is selfish, insensitive gratification, and in *retrospect* we usually know without question when it's been present as we look back on some period or series of incidents in our lives. But it's not always so easy to recognize lust when it's just beginning its destructive work. The reason is that lust tends to hide at first behind what I call one of the seven veils of lustful behavior. These veils, which are described below, are warning signals that we must heed if we hope to defeat lust before it gets started with its destructive work.

The Workaholic Veil.

A workaholic is a person who's never satisfied unless there's more work to be done. For this man or woman, work becomes the ultimate focus and purpose in life. In short, workaholism usually indicates a lust for work that subordinates marriage and family concerns and demands first priority. This kind of lust may hide behind the oft-repeated rationale "I'm doing all this for *us*"—i.e, the family. But in fact, the driving motivation is a lust for money, power, position, or just plain busy-work.

The Pleasure Veil.
The goal here is to "realize my potential," or to "feel good now," or to "enjoy life to the hilt." The person driven by this type of lust may flow from one source of perceived pleasure to another—sex, drugs, food, or whatever. Those in this category are impulsive and undisciplined when the object of their desire becomes available. They're going to overindulge whenever they get the chance. Usually, though, they'll know they've gone too far when guilt sweeps over them. A major characteristic of this type of lust is that it undercuts the ability to defer immediate satisfaction for more rewarding, long-range goals.

The Television Veil.
When you get engrossed in a TV program, it can give the illusion that you've been around the world, performed great feats, and achieved monumental success—all without any effort expended! It's no wonder psychologists and other pundits have begun to refer to compulsive television watching as addictive.

Certainly, TV has its merits, but when it's viewed in excess, the tube can take over a person's life. I even encountered one family who tied their TV into a wall switch so that as soon as they entered the living room and turned on the lights, the TV came on as well! Their lust had become second nature, almost a mechanistic kind of experience. The television had so taken over their lives that they chose not to exercise any control over it at all.

In this case, there was almost no meaningful conversation during the evening between husband and wife, and soon they began to drift apart. Also, very subtly, their basic values and habits seemed to be coming more and more under the influence of the tube. For example, the husband found he was falling into using the jargon favored by some of the characters on one adventure program.

My solution was just to tell them in no uncertain terms to unhook the TV from the light switch and then exercise conscious control over *each* program they watched. Also, we built in some time each evening for them to talk to one another without the intrusion of the tube. It only took a week or so for their relationship to get back on the right track.

The Veil of Conversational Malnutrition.

If you can't carry on a meaningful, civil conversation with your spouse, that's a sign that one of you may be confronting, or on the verge of confronting, problems with lust.

Often, we get involved in lustful activities because there's something wrong with our human relationships, and especially with the marriage relationship. For example, an unsatisfying, boring, or too infrequent sexual relationship may cause one or both spouses to begin to look for outside outlets. And this lack of satisfaction may first emerge in problems in conversation between the partners.

If the individual is only *thinking* about being unfaithful, the irritability that often accompanies indecisiveness may get in the way of satisfying talk with a spouse. On the other hand, if a person is already involved in an extramarital relationship, feelings of guilt may make it hard to engage in deep, meaningful discussions.

In short, being a good spouse means being able to engage in positive, constructive conversation. If the conversation isn't there, lust may very well be.

The Veil of Off-Color Jokes and Language.

Dirty jokes or even seemingly harmless references by a person to infidelity may reflect an intensifying of lust in life. If a person is considering being unfaithful or is in the process of being tempted by some man or woman outside the marriage, he probably won't mention explicitly how his extramarital thoughts and probes are progressing. But he may be signaling indirectly that something lustful is in the works as he is drawn more into sexually oriented talk.

The Graphic Movie Veil.
Movies that emphasize sex, crime, and violence—and many do seem to fall into one of those categories these days—may attract people who are heading steadily in a more lustful direction. These individuals may not have reached the point where they want to act out their fantasies, but they clearly want to be stimulated in certain lustful directions, and films are the easiest way to take the first step.

The Veil of Published Pollution.
Magazines don't have to be outright pornography to get a person thinking in directions that can be unproductive to a marriage. We've become so permissive in our society that it's acceptable to have publications around the home that depict men and women, including many celebrities, dressed in provocative, revealing costumes. It is even considered necessary to expose readers to models who are partially or totally nude—as long as it's done in the name of "art."

Now, I realize it may seem hopelessly old-fashioned and prudish to speak out against such trends. But I feel no need to apologize. We've headed so quickly down the road of permissiveness and amorality in the past two decades that I think we're in danger of completely losing any sense of absolute standards and values. And the problem begins for each of us when we say that it's not necessary to try to control the direction of our lustful fantasies.

So I recommend that you don't fall into the trap of looking at magazines or other literature just because society says it's all right. Rather, search your own libido and determine for yourself what titillates you and what doesn't. If you tend to get turned on sexually by certain kinds of pictures or writing, I'd stay away from them. It's a slippery slope from reading about something or looking at it to taking the first of a series of steps to *doing* it.

Reading matter that suggests lustful thoughts of any type (and that can mean sex, wealth, power, or anything else) starts out by desensitizing you. At first, you may get a kind of kick, which remains in the realm of fantasy. But then you find you need more intense stimulation, and that's when fantasy may turn into action.

But this requires some more thought and discussion. So now, let's turn our focus from the veils that may mask lust to the real dangers to your marriage of lust—the inexorable movement from lustful fantasy to unfaithful reality.

Fantasy: The Window to Real-Life Lust

I can still remember my mother saying to me when I was just a young boy, "Use your imagination, Paul!" She wanted me to learn to think freely about various ways I might act, because she knew that dreams are the stuff reality and achievement are made of.

Lustful adult fantasies work on much the same principle. In a very real sense, our fantasies are the windows that show us the way to more concrete lustful acts and relationships. They're a way of viewing the world as we wish it were, and also as we plan to make it. They reveal exactly what preoccupies us and what our priorities would be if only we were in complete control of our lives.

But at this point, let me make an important distinction between *fantasizing,* on the one hand, and more constructive, future-oriented mental exercises, on the other. For example, there's the very helpful process that Dr. Robert H. Schuller has called *possibility thinking.* Simply stated, possibility thinking is a procedure where in a positive, "can-do" frame of mind, you set a goal, do some intelligent planning, and then apply your talents and beliefs to achieve the end you seek.

Say, for instance, that you want to be a dentist. You can't sit around and just *pretend* you're a dentist and hope to experience any real satisfaction. So you go to school, study hard, and finally you graduate and become a dentist. All the while, you're visualizing success by using your imagination as an instrument of inspiration to move you unswervingly toward your goal.

That's the positive, constructive side of using your imagination. In contrast, mere fantasizing can lead to activity of a very different nature, mostly because it's rooted in lust. When you fantasize, you may visualize participating in a certain activity. But this time, the activity is one that is more likely to be destructive than constructive. Also, there's no discipline or focus in the way most fantasies occur. They pop into your mind and proceed to lead you off on a wild goose chase, which usually causes you to end up far from the real goals you want to achieve.

One man who came to me for help was facing a shattered marriage and frustration in his career goals—all because he had allowed his fantasies to run wild. He had dreamed of being wealthy since he was a child, but fantasy soon overcame his better judgment. He fell into the habit of not setting goals and of failing to work step by step toward his ultimate objective of financial security. Instead, he just followed his fantasies from one immediate gratification to another.

Because he was quite intelligent and got a decent education, he was able to land a series of good jobs in his twenties. But every time he got a little extra money, he went out and bought expensive cars or went with his wife on luxurious vacations. He simply couldn't wait to enjoy the "better things of life."

Also, he soon realized that he would never become rich as quickly as he wanted in a salaried position, so he started playing with entrepreneurial schemes and risky investments. Of course, he never took time to study and plan for these private business ventures—he was too busy fantasizing about where they would eventually take him. As a result, he lost even more money.

The problem was that he had turned into a kind of Toad, from Kenneth Grahame's story *The Wind in the Willows*. Practically anything new or fascinating that crossed his path would catch his fantasy, and he would be off pursuing a mania that had the potential to wreck his entire life.

In short, this man simply couldn't afford his fantasies, and soon he was so deep in debt he had no chance of getting out on his own. A lust for luxury had clouded his better judgment, and he began consistently to spend money when he didn't have it.

At one point, he got so far into a financial hole that he had to declare bankruptcy. Also, he lost job after job because he consistently got into disagreements with his bosses. His main problem was that he was totally frustrated that he wasn't moving ahead more rapidly toward his goal of great wealth.

All these financial problems finally placed his marriage in jeopardy, and in desperation the couple sought me out. After several sessions, we traced the problem back to his unbridled fantasies about wealth and position. The answer to this man's problems was to put him on a strict, practical, step-by-step "recovery" program from his fantasy life. I actually *forbade* him to act on his fantasies for a period of several months.

"I know it's going to be hard," I told him. "But you've got to start disciplining your mind. Your problems start in your mind, because first you come up with some wild desire or scheme. Then you begin to live your fantasy without really thinking through the consequences. So you've got to stop this process before it even gets started."

Even though their relationship had become strained, he

and his wife were able to talk freely with one another. So I encouraged him to tell her as soon as a fantasy came into his mind. A practical woman, she served as a "reality check" for him: As long as she knew what was going on in his mind, she was in a position to poke holes in the most outrageous schemes and deflate the crazy ideas before her husband began to act on them.

In this man's case, fantasy became synonymous with lust, or a drive toward immediate, self-serving gratification. And the temptation to fantasize was so deeply ingrained that it took a while for his way of thinking to change. But at least we managed to put the brakes on his actions until his lustful thoughts dissipated and his imagination turned in more realistic, healthy directions.

But what about sexual fantasies? I've suggested that all lustful thinking—including sexual lust—may lead to destructive acting out of the fantasy. But is that really true as far as sex is concerned?

As you know, we've been deluged in recent years by a wave of advice from sex researchers, pop psychologists, and other pundits who promote the benefits of sexual fantasies. There's a tendency to consider most if not all erotic fantasies as normal, even including those that involve violent or sadistic behavior. The argument goes like this: Whatever stimulates your libido is good for you! It's fun! It's perfectly all right as long as it doesn't lead to destructive action—and there's no reason it should lead to such action.

I couldn't disagree more. Time after time, I've encountered people who were victims of a danger of sexual fantasy, which I call the sexual domino effect. Here's how it works:

Sexual Domino #1:
You begin to fantasize about some sort of illicit, extramarital sex. This could happen after you take in information of stimulation—such as through the movies, television, soft-core magazines, or some other outside source. Or you might just

take a "mental trip" back to some old love affair or to some other sexually stimulating incident.

Sexual Domino #2:
You become preoccupied for periods of time with lust and fantasy so that you begin to engage in self-gratification. Even when you have sex with your mate, you usually rely on a fantasy to turn you on. Your spouse is no longer as involved in your sex life.

Sexual Domino #3:
Your sexual fantasy life and periods of self-gratification increase in scope, mainly because you're becoming desensitized. The initial pleasure you got from your fantasies just isn't enough anymore.

Sexual Domino #4:
You begin to look for more sexual excitement outside the home. It may be more voyeurism than direct involvement at first—such as going to porno movies or live sex shows.

Sexual Domino #5:
Finally, looking just can't satisfy you anymore, so you decide the time has come to take a little action. Now, you've reached the point where you're ripe for having an extramarital relationship. Often only half-consciously, you begin to look for opportunities; and sure enough, they begin to come your way. It may be a one-night stand on a business trip; or you may move right into a full-blown affair with some available person in the neighborhood or at work. However it happens, you've taken the decisive step of moving from fantasy to actual infidelity.

Now, I realize that many times, people don't go through all these dominoes. But still, many times they do. In my counseling experience, an extramarital sex act is rarely the first expression of the lust in a person's life. On the contrary, it's usually the *last.* The consummated infidelity occurs only after a number of those other dominoes have tumbled down.

Jesus summed this process up rather well in his Sermon on the Mount: "You have heard that it was said, 'You shall not commit adultery.' But I say to you that everyone who looks at a woman lustfully has already committed adultery with her in his heart."

Some argue, of course, that extramarital "love," for them, had nothing to do with lust. They say it was a romantic impulse, completely unplanned. I say, Hogwash! I've found that in almost every case there's a period of preparation and an increasing level of lustful fantasizing before an actual affair. So stop the process before it even gets started! Recognize those sexual fantasies for what they are: the first rituals in an increasingly powerful movement toward infidelities that could leave your marriage in shambles.

Of course, it's not always so easy to change the direction of your fantasies and to head off an impulse toward infidelity. Lust is a powerful force that is rooted deeply in our selfish, rebellious nature. Indeed, the basic difference between lust and love seems to be that the first is self-directed while the second is other-directed.

So I know it would be wonderful if I could tell you that the lust in your life will evaporate into thin air, never to haunt you again, if you just take a few simple steps to get rid of it. And sometimes, through a powerful personal experience with God, this may indeed happen.

But more often, the lust gets eliminated through what the Bible calls a process of sanctification—or being made holier and purer as you draw closer to God. In other words, what we're talking about here doesn't usually involve quick-fix solutions. Old, pleasurable habits die hard. There may even be withdrawal pains.

But if you seek help from your spouse in opposing your fantasies—or from some other close confidant if you just feel it would be hurtful to discuss some matters with your spouse

—your chances for success will be greatly enhanced. And if you can also bring God, through prayer, into the process of changing and uprooting those destructive lusts, that's even better. I can tell you from my own experience that with you, your spouse, and God working together, you'll virtually assure your chances of success in observing this seventh commandment.

THE EIGHTH COMMANDMENT

Swing into a Slow-Motion Style

As much as I hate to admit it, at least once a day I fall victim to the "rush-rush" syndrome.

In a typical scenario, my morning usually starts pleasantly enough. But an unexpected phone call may put me a little behind schedule. Then I come up with a lecture idea that hadn't dawned on me before, so I spend a couple of extra minutes working it through, to be sure I have all my thoughts put together properly.

Now I'm really running late. So I have to rush to the university or risk being tardy for a class. But, of course, the traffic lights are all against me this morning. So I drive a little faster than I should and hope desperately I'll find a parking place near my classroom. Unfortunately, I have to park farther away than usual, and that means an extra minute or so of walking.

I begin to jog toward my classroom, with the minutes ticking away, spurred on by visions of restless students wondering what happened to the teacher. I do manage to make it in to the classroom just on time, but there's a film of perspiration on my forehead, my breath is coming a little hard, and my thinking is anything but composed.

Fortunately, I usually have at least a couple of minutes to compose myself and collect my scattered thoughts before I launch into a lecture. But on those occasions when I'm running late, I get angry at myself. And I usually renew a long-standing commitment to try to slow my life down. It's no fun to rush about like that. It's also not very healthy to allow my schedule to get so out of whack that a lack of time begins to wreak havoc on my nerves and increase my stress levels.

But let's face it. For most of us, the rush-rush syndrome is an ongoing fact of life. We're a society governed by the clock, as we get bombarded from every direction by demands on our time. Our culture actually encourages a frenetic pace and a keen sense of urgency. On television, for example, they blitz us with commercial messages in fifteen, thirty, or sixty seconds. In those short segments of time, the advertiser hits us with an incredible amount of information and sales pressure: Here's why you should identify with our product . . . buy our product . . . watch our product change the quality of your life.

We are confronted with the challenge of taking in all this information, analyzing it, and making a decision, all in a matter of seconds. Then we're off and running in a new direction. In our highly stimulated society, we're constantly tempted to dance to the rhythm of a clock, and that makes it easy to become preoccupied with the variety of outside stimulation.

But where does a marriage fit into all this hyperactivity?

Sometimes, unless we consciously devise a strategy to slow down, our marriage may not fit in at all. One of two things is likely to happen.

First, one spouse may simply be crowded out of the other's life. Work, television, or any of countless other sources of stimulation may take control of the time of one or both partners. They may pass like the proverbial ships in the night, hardly acknowledging the presence of the other.

The second result of unbridled rushing about is more difficult to detect. This involves togetherness without true communion. You and your spouse may participate in common interests; you may share dinners with friends and attend business functions together; you may even make sure you're both active in your church or synagogue.

But still, even if you're spending the time together, you may not really be participating in these activities with a real sense of oneness and unity. In other words, each may be vaguely aware of the presence of the other. But the activities and the presence of outsiders can get in the way of mutual admiration, reflection, and affirmation.

One way to slow down your life and begin to enjoy the quiet presence of each other more is just to set aside some time for talk and reflection after an activity. Say, you go to a concert. When you arrive home, the chances are you won't discuss and savor the experience you've just had. Rather, one of you will turn on the television to catch the late news. Or your children will hear you and want to say a lengthy good night.

Now, I'm not saying there's anything inherently wrong with watching the news or tucking in the kids. But there is a problem if these activities and responsibilities crowd out quality time you and your spouse might be spending together. Any good intentions about setting aside slow-down times will almost always get postponed or lost completely unless you get tough and build in a definite time when you and your spouse can sit down alone together.

That may mean refusing to turn on the TV at all or telling the kids, after a *brief* good night, "Now, Daddy and I want to spend a little time together, and you need to get your rest. So let's go on to sleep, okay?"

It's necessary sometimes just to draw the line with our other activities and relationships—and that includes our relationships with our children. Sound a little tough? Well, it *is* tough for many parents to discipline their use of time so that they allow themselves time alone with each other outside the presence of the kids. There are always reservations and guilt feelings that may well up in such cases: We should have gone in to give Johnny two extra glasses of water this evening . . . we were selfish, thinking too much of ourselves . . . we won't have that little guy around many more years.

But believe me, as long as you give Johnny sufficient time during the day and on weekends, he'll survive quite well. In fact, you have a responsibility to your marriage to insist on extra time with your spouse in the evening, after Johnny is already supposed to be asleep. Your marriage *demands* this kind of special, first-priority time together. And Johnny needs to know he's not always the center of attention.

Also, that time you set aside for each other should be relaxed and open-ended. The best things in life are typically experienced at a leisurely pace—or in a kind of slow motion, which allows you to relax and savor the moment. It's like the difference between instant tea served in a paper cup and finely brewed spiced tea, delicately steeped and sipped in china cups.

The chances are you learned this slow-motion principle before you got married, but gradually, in the fast-moving pressures of life, you forgot it. Remember those summer evenings walking along leisurely with your sweetheart or sitting on a living room sofa or a porch swing? You just sat and talked and spooned in those days and completely lost track of time.

So why consign these great experiences to memory?

All you have to do is swing into a slow-motion style to recapture those special times. It's a matter of setting things up so that you linger more in the presence of your spouse; you enjoy her; you share intimate secrets and dreams with him; and mostly, you both just savor the time together.

But before you begin to swing into an easier, more relaxed relationship with your spouse, you may find you first have to confront several enemies of the slow-motion style. In particular, I've identified three that commonly plague married cou-

ples. I'd suggest you deal with them decisively before you try
to set up a relaxed time for a renewal of matrimonial communion.

Enemy #1:   Hyped-up speech
A strained, machine-gun style of speaking can be evidence of
underlying anxiety and an excessive sense of urgency. Everyone knows at least a few compulsive talkers. They rattle on at
breakneck speed, often without pausing to hear answers to
their own questions. Sometimes this is just a bad habit.
Sometimes it's an indication that the person isn't interested
in anything other than his own concerns. Most often, though,
it's a cover-up for a fear of confronting one's own inadequacies and inabilities to interact meaningfully with others.

Unfortunately, our culture fuels this kind of speech. Think
again about television commercials. The second they come
on, the volume goes up. Also, much of the hype is from fast-
paced speech and catchy jingles that stick in our minds.
Then, the advertisers use repetition. I know of one commercial for a pain reliever that repeats the same sentence six times
in thirty seconds! The only pain relief *I* need is to escape from
this ridiculous assault on my sensitivities!

Compulsive talkers also expect others to emulate media-
style speech. If you can't make your point in fifteen seconds,
they'll often butt in and finish your sentences for you. Their
sole intent is to get to the heart of the matter of *your* conversation—so that they can get on with their own.

If you find yourself falling into such hyped-up speech patterns, consciously reduce the tempo. Just slowing down your
speech patterns and stepping up your listening will make you
feel more relaxed. And your marriage will begin to gain from
better-balanced conversations.

Enemy #2:   Hyped-up work and household activities
The second enemy of developing a slow-motion style in your
marriage is a tendency always to be on the move, darting here

and there, doing something. There are many possible reasons for this way of operating. For some people, it may be mainly habit. They've gotten used to busy-work, and they wouldn't know what to do if they had to sit still for a few moments.

Others are desperately afraid they'll miss something in life if they don't maintain a hyped-up pace of activities. They are determined that life won't pass them by. So they overcrowd their calendars, schedule wall-to-wall commitments, and the activities begin to crowd out the very essence of the marriage relationship.

The most likely candidates for this pattern of activity are really the ones who should know better: It's those with the highest educational and intelligence levels who are most likely to be seduced by the hyped-activity syndrome. These people often have a high achievement orientation, and they develop a compulsion to do and accomplish more and more. But they're fooling themselves. In reality, they become victims of fragmentation as they squander their energies on everything except what matters most—their relationships, and especially their marriages.

One minister I know is like a lot of other men and women of the cloth. He has a kind of "messiah complex." He thinks the success of his church, which for him is defined by growth in numbers, contributions, and service programs, depends almost entirely on him. In his view, he's the only person with the capacity to do any job really right.

As a result, he has developed a daily regimen that the hardest chargers in a crack combat unit would envy. He's up and moving at the crack of dawn, and his church work and activities in the community fill up the entire day. Then it's home for a quick dinner and back to church for committee meetings far into the night.

And, of course, he doesn't have the weekend off. That's when he really puts his nose to the grindstone. He spends all day Saturday working on his sermon and putting the final touches on the Sunday services. Then on Sundays, he oversees two services and other "churchy" activities. On Monday morning, he's back on the treadmill.

And his family? Yes, he does have a wife and three children. But they rarely see him. His wife has become quite resentful, and he may well be heading toward that tragedy of clergy divorce, which is becoming so rampant in this country. I know about the dangers, because I deal regularly with the divorce issue in counseling sessions with the clergy and their wives.

In this pastor's case, the jury isn't yet in. He and his wife have just started coming in for counseling, and it hasn't yet registered on him what he's doing to himself and his marriage. It's ironic that he has a burning desire to save souls and change the world for the better and at the same time he's allowing his family life to disintegrate.

What this man needs is simply to slow down, cut out 25 percent of his activities, and take more time to relax and be with his wife. It remains to be seen, however, whether or not he'll be able to achieve this goal.

Enemy #3:   Hyped-up entertainment

When it's time to enjoy our leisure hours, there's often an assumption that everything has to be planned in minute detail. Every minute must be accounted for and used to the best advantage. If a husband and wife want to go out together, they may cram their evening full of activities—say, a quick dinner *and* a movie, instead of just dinner *or* a movie.

Also, they may use their leisure time to meet certain social obligations, such as inviting other couples to join them. The result is that they put themselves on a split-second schedule and they fall right into that rush-rush syndrome we mentioned at the beginning of this chapter.

Stimulation and more stimulation becomes the order of the day, rather than using those off hours to relax and enjoy the other spouse's company. Why not just a leisurely dinner for two with nothing else planned? Or how about a walk in the park or some window-shopping?

Your marriage can only become tough and resilient if you take the time to work on it. Leisure hours are the best time, and may be the only time, to tend seriously to your relationship. If you pack that time full of hyped-up entertainment, you and your mate will drift further and further apart.

So these are the three main enemies of most efforts to develop a slow-motion style in marriage. Now, what can you do to combat them? What strategies can you devise that will reduce the level of pressure and stress in the husband-wife relationship? I summarize my approach with five resounding nos and one big yes.

The Five Nos

1. *Say NO to the car radio.* When you're driving anywhere with your spouse—whether to a vacation spot, to church, or to the local shopping center—silence is not just dead air. It's an opportunity to let your two minds mill about, mingle, and finally move together to new insights and commitments. You might even try singing together in the car. Some couples I know find themselves smiling and laughing together for the first time in months during the first such singing session.

2. *Say NO to television.* I know I've said many things against TV in the preceding pages, but the reason I keep returning to this subject is that I see the tube as one of the major threats to developing a tough marriage. The television too easily becomes a subsitute for human company, and especially the company of your spouse.

3. *Say NO to noise pollution.* Sometime, just sit in your favorite chair and listen. The chances are you'll hear noise that is getting in the way of fruitful conversation: It could be the high-fi, our old friend the TV set, the news on the kitchen radio, the banging of pots and pans, the dishwasher, telephone talk, or an argument involving the children.

Whatever the cause, excessive noise amounts to more than simply background clutter. It intrudes on meaningful conversation, relaxation, and concentration on the needs of your spouse. So be sure to stop it or escape to a quieter room before you begin to try to embark on a relaxed talk with your mate.

4. *Say NO to "groupie" outings.* When was the last time you asked your spouse out on a date? Just the two of you—no kids, friends, business associates?

We tend to develop a kind of "groupie complex" as adolescents. For teenagers, it's an unwritten law that you're a freak or at least a little odd if you like to attend movies or other outings alone. And the more people you hang around with, the more popular and desirable you become.

But that way of thinking can be disastrous for a marriage. It's absolutely essential that you and your spouse go off regularly by yourselves, just the two of you, and get to know each other better than you know any other human beings. I know several couples who do this, and I'll explain the approach a little later in this chapter.

5. *Say NO to passive living.* By passive living I mean being a person who moves through life haphazardly, reacting primarily to the pressures and stimulations of the moment and following the flow of fads and current trends. Those who live this way exercise no control over their destiny. Their values are the values of the moment; they have no independent criteria to aid them in planning where their individual lives—and their marriages—are going.

The antidote to a passive marriage is simply to take the bull by the horns and become an activist in directing the course of your relationship. That means sitting down with your spouse and planning where you want to be a year, two years, and five years from now.

As you put together this action plan, you need to consider every aspect of your marital and family activity: Are you eating together often enough? Having meaningful vacations? Getting involved in joint projects? Having enough fun in each other's company? If your answer to any of these questions is no, then to one degree or another, you're probably a victim of passive living.

These, then, are five dangers or "enemies" that I recommend couples keep in mind in developing a more relaxing relationship. But your movement toward a slow-motion life style isn't limited to negatives. In addition to these five nos, there is also a big, resounding *yes*, which is the most important factor of all.

The Big Yes

The big yes in the most relaxed, easy-going, and enjoying marital relationships is what I call fallow time. *Fallow* literally means to lie dormant or idle, and it's a concept that has been applied most often to the land.

Before the days of sophisticated technology, back in biblical times and even earlier, farmers used a rotation system of seven-year periods to revitalize their fields. For six years they would plant and harvest, but during the seventh year, the field was allowed to lie fallow.

The fallow year was a time of rest for the soil, a time to replenish and nourish. And originally, the concept didn't involve any active intervention in the land. There was no rotation of crops. There wasn't any injection of fertilizers and stimulants. Rather, the rejuvenation came from a lack of activity.

The practice of the seventh fallow year echoes the original notion of the Sabbath. You'll recall that on the seventh day, after six days of creation, God "caught his breath." Likewise, on the Sabbath day we catch our breath, through worship, rest, and service. And in the seventh year, the soil catches *its* breath by lying uncultivated for a time.

This is the basic concept that we need to build into our
marriages. After we cram our minds full of information and
knowledge and fill our days with activity and projects, we
need to provide for some fallow time and space in our lives
and closest relationships.

But in practical terms how do we go about this?

A sabbatical every seven years in a marriage obviously
won't do the trick. Instead, we need to include some fallow
time *daily*, where spouses just get off by themselves and enjoy
one another quietly, without any particular purpose or agenda
other than being together.

As I've mentioned before, I know some married couples
who have built formal dates into their relationship. In one instance, a husband and wife without children fell into the
habit of eating in their apartment and then, immediately af-
terward, turning on the evening news. Many times, they
would begin their meal close to the time for the news to
begin. So they never had a chance to get involved in any significant conversation before their attention had become riv-
eted on the tube. Then, each would get involved in errands or
duties around the apartment, and before they realized it, bedtime had arrived.

This young couple knew something was wrong. They knew
they were falling into a rut. But at first they couldn't figure
out what to do about it. At one point, they sensed they were
drifting so far apart that some sort of therapy sessions seemed
in order.

But then they heard a lecture *on television* about how
married couples were losing the ability to communicate with
one another because they never gave themselves any time to
practice talking to one another. Suddenly, something clicked
in the husband's mind.

"I think what we need is just to start talking to each
other," he said. "But let's face it, we can't even get started in
this apartment."

"So why don't we go out?" his wife suggested.

The upshot was that they decided it would be cheaper to go out to an inexpensive local restaurant three or four nights a week than to pay for the services of a therapist. And as it turned out, the relaxed, fallow time they established for communion with one another paid off immediately in a more enjoyable and exciting relationship.

In the last analysis, slowing down your life means simplifying it. To find fallow time, you'll most likely have to cut out some activity or commitment. The one you'll choose to eliminate will probably be something that's been pushing you "over the edge" or causing you to succumb to the anxiety-producing pressures of modern life.

When you take that step toward quietness and rest in the company of your spouse, you may well find that your marriage responds like the lands of the ancient Hebrews. The time off will rejuvenate and nurture the two of you and move you toward a more complete state of unity and oneness. And that's what swinging into a slow-motion style in your marriage is really all about.

THE NINTH
COMMANDMENT

Prepare for the Pits Instead of the Peaks

Jesus on the Mount of Transfiguration.

Moses on Mount Sinai.

The so-called "mountaintop experience" is deeply embedded in our most meaningful spiritual and relational encounters. It's a time of supreme insight, joy, and inner development. Yet it only lasts for a moment. Then it becomes a supportive memory that sustains us as we make the inevitable descent back into the valleys—and even the pits—of daily life.

Most people are realistic enough to understand that the course of life will always include some hills and valleys. But the picture we paint of marriage, especially when we're first starting out, is always somewhat romanticized. It's true that the hills are sometimes going to be exhilarating, uplifting peak experiences. But at the same time, some of the valleys may only be properly described as the "pits." These are terrible and even tragic events that we'd really rather not even think about. But the only way to build an enduring, tough marriage is to prepare thoroughly for those pits even as we enjoy the peaks to the hilt.

The first step in getting ready is to avoid the pitfalls of wishful thinking. Just recognize, right out front, that you and your spouse eventually are going to face some serious problems in your marriage. As you try to become more realistic, it helps to be aware of some of the forces in our society that create problems for our marriages. Although these forces can be overcome, it takes a tough marriage to do it. Now, let me opine about two negative cultural forces I consider to be especially threatening to a marriage.

Cultural Force #1: Marriage in the eighties is suffering from an overdose of secular values.
Unfortunately, our cultural and societal values don't often support strong, long-term marriage relationships. Here are some of the most insidious anti-marriage forces I've encountered in my own counseling work:

- *"Self" is sacred.* It all comes down to the old notion of looking out for number one above all else. That's the antithesis of the pedestal relationship we talked about under the first commandment. Much of our culture is designed to enhance self-development, or to put *me* at the center of the universe. So, there's a tendency when we get married to ask "what's in it for me?" and that can be a deadly attitude.
- *Marriage remains only an option and therefore is always expendable.* This notion can be restated like this: It was my choice to make this commitment, and so it's my right to break it. Increasing numbers of people are carrying this option concept to its logical conclusion in a variety of ways. They may just choose to enjoy the benefits of marriage without the traditional "strings," as they live together without religious or civil sanction. Or they may regard one or more divorces as one of the inevitable and natural "passages" of life. This cavalier attitude just puts marriage in the category of another disposable commodity.

• *Marriage is just an emotional sideline—a supplement to my real interests in life.* This secular assumption completely eliminates the idea of real commitment in marriage. The matrimonial bond becomes an emotional and sexual convenience, not a relationship that can bring true character and meaning into your life.

Tough marriage in the sense I'm talking about it in this book is severely at odds with these secular notions. Marriage is a sacred union, a uniting of two as one. Most important of all, it's conceived and sanctioned by God himself. So marriage isn't there just as a convenience or to make you feel good. It isn't intended as a commodity you try on for size or throw away when it wears out.

At the most basic level, marriage is a reverent commitment, a vow to endure the pits even as you enjoy the peaks. But if you try to build your marriage on the basis of any of these secular assumptions we've considered, you're very likely to bail out when you confront the pits. Your relationship just won't be tough enough to enable you to meet the major challenges head-on and emerge victorious.

Cultural Force #2: An overwhelming number of American couples marry for the wrong reasons.
Historically, the most viable marriages have been firmly rooted in practical considerations. In the past, many married mainly to guarantee their rightful place in society or to achieve financial security. Parents or guardians commonly prearranged such unions, with little regard for the feelings of the bride and groom. Even when the prospective spouses have had a choice, there has still been a tendency to get married for pragmatic reasons. For example, many people would just get the urge to settle down and raise a family, and marriage was a necessary first step. If you wanted to live with a person of the opposite sex and have children—*and* wanted the acceptance of your local community—you had to take the

proper marriage vows. Others might get married for financial security, physical protection, or social position.

And once marriages occurred, they tended to be permanent. After all, what better alternatives were there? Divorce was very difficult to obtain, and a divorced person often found it hard, if not impossible, to get remarried because of the social stigma of divorce. So the "till death do us part" clause in the marriage ceremony really had some teeth to it.

In our own day, however, we're playing a different ball game. Old-fashioned marriage has taken a back seat to new concepts of personal independence and also a radical acceptance of the supremacy of romance. Greater job opportunities for women have enabled them to pick up and leave a relationship they don't like. The Love Boat is waiting to whisk any couple away for an intimate interlude, with no questions asked about marital status. The secular media constantly sanction, explicitly or implicitly, such practices as cohabitation, adultery, premarital sex, and giving birth out of wedlock.

In short, marriage no longer occupies the key historic role that it once did. Instead, it's been relegated to just another emotional support system, which isn't necessarily tied in to deep-rooted spiritual and societal values.

It's really incredible when you think about it. For perhaps the first time in history, an entire society has become intent on marrying primarily for emotional reasons. Now we speak of how we *feel* about our mate; how we *feel* about the relationship; how we *feel* about our mutual inner needs.

Don't misunderstand me: I'm not suggesting that you should forget about your emotions. On the contrary, it's important to get them out on the table with your spouse and deal effectively with them. The problem I see is that marriages these days are often based mostly or solely on feelings. But feelings alone can't prepare and *steel* you for the abrupt downturns that your marriage is bound to take.

In this regard, I recall one couple that started out as starry-eyed as any I've ever encountered. They just *knew*, beyond any question, that they had been destined for each other since the beginning of time. And they began their marriage with the assumption that the sweet-talking, hand-holding, billing-and-cooing courtship they had experienced would continue until the day they left this world in tandem, in their eighties or nineties.

In fact, their romantic natures, freedom from financial worries (they were both well paid in their jobs), and freedom from family concerns (no children so far) helped them preserve this blissful state well beyond the honeymoon trip.

But then, about two years into their marriage, the young wife was struck by cancer of the breast. A mastectomy had to be performed, and all the worry-free euphoria quickly evaporated. Now the emotional pendulum had swung against them. The wife was constantly depressed because she didn't see how her husband could love her anymore. Also, she was too "down" to return to work immediately. Her spouse also got depressed because the image he had constructed in his mind of how their life should proceed had been completely shattered. As his wife had feared, he found he wasn't capable of regarding her in the same romantic way that he had before.

Unfortunately, this husband and wife didn't have any solid resources to fall back on. Their marriage had definitely plunged into one of those pits, and they didn't have the power to propel it out again. Within a year they had filed for divorce, and both had to go into therapy to deal with the guilt feelings and sense of failure and disappointment they experienced.

So you can see why I've said that emotions and feelings are simply an unreliable foundation for a tough and resilient relationship. But how can you prepare for pits like these before they trap you and destroy your marriage?

My approach here is the precise opposite of what I've recommended elsewhere in this book. In short, instead of thinking positively at this point, I want you to indulge in a veritable binge of *negative thinking*.

Try Some Negative Thinking

Just as physical exercise can keep your body in condition, certain mental exercises can help prepare and strengthen you to confront inner challenges. One approach that I've found to be quite helpful is what some call the *worst-case scenario*. Stated simply, the idea is first to imagine the worst thing or things that could possibly happen to you. Then, begin to work them through in your mind, on paper, and in prayer until you come up with some tentative solutions.

Finally, I think it's a good idea to jot down those solutions for later reference if the dire event you've imagined ever does arise. And most important of all, after you finish this worst-case speculation, you should immediately begin to work on weaknesses you've uncovered in your character, spiritual development, and relationship with your spouse.

Specifically, here's a step-by-step procedure I recommend to root out the worst pits or ruts that could cause your marriage to stumble. The idea is to let your imagination range over all these unpleasant possibilities. Then, once you've imagined yourself in these terrible situations, the rest is up to you: You'll have to decide, given your own personality and value system, how you might climb out of these deep valleys of marital despair.

Worst Case #1:   You both lose your jobs.
Perhaps you're laid off or fired, or the company goes out of business. The chances are this won't happen to both of you at the same time if you both have jobs; but after all, we're talking about worst cases here! Also, if you *are* both working, it's likely you're also living well beyond one of your incomes. It would really hurt to lose one of those sources of money, wouldn't it? So just imagine how much more devastating it would be if you *both* found yourselves out of work.

But press on: carry the scenario a little further. Unemployment is running at a high rate in your field. Your savings are dwindling fast. One of your children is about to enter college.

And *you* have to foot all the bills. What are you going to do?

Now, we approach a true worst-case test. Suppose there are jobs available that don't pay as well as your old one and certainly don't carry anywhere near the same prestige? Are you willing to lower your sights?

What's going on inside of you by this time? Is your sense of personal identity slipping away? Are you going to get irritable and be tempted to lash out at your mate? Is there any chance you'll seek solace outside your marital relationship?

What about your spouse: Do you expect she will start taking all the trouble very hard? What are you going to say or do to support her (or him)?

I realize this sort of speculation can be quite nerve-racking, and you may well ask, "Why put myself through this until I have to?" My answer is that this sort of negative thinking is essential to long-range planning and growth in a marriage. It's quite likely that things are not always going to go completely smoothly in life. So if you can do a little anticipating—and in the process, ask God to show you how to deal with possible problems—you'll be a much stronger and better prepared mate. And your marriage will be much more likely to survive the pits.

Worst Case #2:   You lose your home.
You have a house, condo, or rented apartment—and suddenly you find yourself facing life without a roof over your head. It could be as a result of fire, mortgage foreclosure, or simply a lack of rent money. What are you going to do about it, and how are you and your spouse going to take this crisis?

Another way of putting this is: How much of your identity is tied up in a piece of property? How much of your concern is related simply to shelter, and how much is tied up in status? Be honest with yourself at this point. The more concern you have for status, the harder it's going to be for you to let a particular dwelling go—and the more likely it is that the worries and anxieties will put an unbearable burden on your marriage.

There are also a number of variations on this theme: Suppose you find that you can't "trade up" to that dream house you always wanted. Your family income just doesn't permit it. What's that going to do to your sense of self-worth?

Then, suppose one of you is completely disabled or dies. Will the other have enough money in insurance or savings to continue the mortgage payments or rent? Would the lack of a financial cushion in the face of such a tragedy put an excessive strain on you? Don't answer these questions lightly. Think them through, and then follow up with some probing questions of your own.

Worst Case #3:   You have no car.
This could happen in several ways. Suppose your car breaks down and you can't use it for several days or even weeks. Most people can survive that, but it could put a strain on a family if you have no back-up plan.

The worst case of all, of course, would be if you found you couldn't afford a car at all. Or if you found you had to drive one that was so broken down that you were embarrassed to be seen by friends in it.

It may seem strange, but this presents a real trauma for many men I've counseled. We live in a culture where quite a few people consider cars an ultimate status symbol. How much of your self-concept or ego is wrapped up in the form of transportation you use?

Worst Case #4:   You can't afford, or temporarily lose the use of, your favorite electronic gadgets.
For many people, it's hard to imagine life without television, a stereo, a radio, and perhaps a video cassette recorder. We're addicted to the entertainment they provide. But what would happen in your home if your favorite gadget, say the TV, broke down, and at the time you simply couldn't afford another—or you decide you won't repair it?

For several years I've served as a host for a Holy Land tour that leaves the States right after Christmas and returns from

Israel shortly into the New Year. In talking with prospective tour members, I stress an unusual but important benefit of that particular tour: "You'll miss all the holiday season college football bowl games and the NFL playoffs! And you'll return to the USA refreshed and renewed—in part because you've avoided the holiday TV overdose!"

So far, all tour members have, upon their return, remarked how wonderful it was to begin the New Year without the burden of TV sports-viewing burn-out. It's ironic that a major joy of going to the Holy Land over New Year's is the discovery you don't have to watch TV.

Here, we should refer to an earlier discussion of noise pollution. Most of our favorite electronic gadgets involve some sort of noise. So a key question we have to consider is, How would you and your spouse deal with the extra quiet?

It's important, by the way, to distinguish between quiet and void. Quiet is the opportunity for creative listening between you and your spouse. Void is noncreative nothingness. Because most people don't know how to treat silence as creative quiet, they treat it as a void and try to fill it up with noise. But the odd thing is, if you plan ahead, you can easily accept the absence of noise and discover just how creative silence can be. In fact, you may decide, after thinking through this particular worst-case scenario, to bring it on without waiting for it!

Worst Case #5:   There's not enough money for new clothes. How would you feel if you always had to buy low-priced clothes from the cheapest retail store in your area? No more high-fashion designer dresses or suits. Or suppose you had to sell your favorite coat or go a couple of seasons without buying any new clothing?

Honestly now, how far back could you cut your clothes budget because of a cash squeeze and not go around moping or take it out on your spouse? I know one young wife who confessed she absolutely has to have some jazzy new clothes at least once every four months. Otherwise, she begins to slip into her bad mood and starts thinking of herself as dowdy. She knows herself well enough to sense these negative feelings coming on a week or so in advance, and she's quite a hard person to live with until this sartorial urge is satisfied.

Fortunately, she and her husband have been able to afford this indulgence so far. But what will happen if they find they can no longer afford this luxury? A job crisis or an extra child will require some real changes in their spending habits and values. And I wonder quite seriously how their relationship would fare if she weren't able to purchase the latest fashions.

My advice to this couple has been to spend an hour or so together focusing on this particular worst-case scenario. The wife hasn't yet completely conquered this weakness of hers, but at least she's taking a closer look at how unhealthy it is for her sense of self to be so wrapped up in what she wears.

Worst Case #6:   One of you loses your health.
Now we're moving beyond financial questions to some of the most disturbing, health-and-death issues. When one or the other of you gets very sick, that's certainly going to affect your finances. If the spouse who is ill usually contributes substantially or solely to the family income, the financial strain gets even worse.

But perhaps the most difficult factor is that a loss of health will create a new role for each spouse. You'll have to ask yourself an entirely new set of questions about your basic relationship: Can you lovingly, patiently, and consistently offer *perpetual* care and support? Or if the shoe is on the other foot, can you lovingly, openly, and unselfishly *accept* that care and support?

If you're the kind of person who tends to reject affection or assistance—in other words, if you are exceptionally independent and self-sufficient—you'll have to get prepared to change some of your personal traits. Also, if you need a great deal of attention and "babying" but then find it's your spouse who now needs all the help and assistance, that can impose some big personal demands on you.

In the last analysis, a loss of health will require both mates to adjust. And I find that the best way to prepare for a major adjustment is to play through this negative scenario in your mind.

Worst Case #7: *You lose your spouse to death.*
This may seem to be going too far. After all, if you're happily married, why make yourself unhappy by contemplating such disasters?

Also, some may argue that all this pessimistic thinking may lead a person into some sort of self-fulfilling prophecy. In other words, thinking and pondering about hard times ahead may actually cause them to happen.

Let me say first of all that I don't for a moment believe that this exercise we're going through will cause any of these bad things to happen. And I don't think you do either, unless you happen to be considerably more superstitious than most people.

But at the same time, I do think a *constructive* kind of self-fulfilling prophecy may arise from this worst-case scenario. That is, if you think through any of these terrible scenarios, you'll be in a better position to handle the real thing when and if it occurs. I can predict or prophesy with some certainty that there will be benefits in the future from this worst-case approach.

First, let's focus on the possibility of terminal illness. As a practical matter, it's very likely that one of you will die before the other. In fact, the longer-living spouse may well have to go through an emotionally wrenching period of watching the other partner slip away.

Now, I'll be the first to acknowledge that it's virtually impossible for most people to imagine what this tragedy would be like—and to anticipate precisely how they might respond. One husband I know says, "I feel certain I don't have the strength in myself to deal with the death of my wife. The only way I'd make it would be with God's help."

And that's just the point. Many people would feel inadequate to shoulder the burden of caring for a dying spouse. In fact, they *would* be incapable of handling such a problem all by themselves. Hence, it's essential to begin *now* to build personal and spiritual support systems that will provide reservoirs of strength when those tough times do occur.

Understand, though, I'm not trying to manipulate you into "getting religion." Nor am I suggesting that you gather a cadre of supportive friends around you merely to ensure that you'll have help at some undetermined point in the future. Obviously, true spirituality and genuine friendships have a much broader *raison d'être* than that.

But at the same time, using the worst-case approach, you can begin now to get some idea of the future importance of a present relationship with God and with other human beings. When a person begins to think in detail about future possibilities—especially threatening ones, like death—that can be a powerful motivator to change present attitudes and actions.

So, by projecting your present spirituality and friendships into the future, you can begin to get some idea of how well prepared you may be to confront catastrophe. By the same token, if you *fail* to engage in any such present imaginings about the future, it's likely you'll be caught with meager inner and outer resources to cope when tragedy strikes.

The husband I mentioned above, who said he was certain he would be inadequate to deal with the death of his wife, actually began to probe this particular worst-case scenario in his deepest thoughts and prayers. He jotted down his reactions and even drew up a rough checklist of actions he might take if his wife discovered she had only a few months to live.

"I confronted my fears head-on and tried to think of practical ways I could manage if my wife died," he said. "And I found that the fears tended to subside. They didn't disappear.

I don't want to suggest that. But I did find I could at least think about her death calmly and rationally, without wanting to run away in the opposite direction. And you know what? I discovered that I started living more intensely each day with my wife. I appreciate her more and I'm thankful for all she contributes to our home."

I think this last point may be the most important of all. As I mentioned, I'm not by nature a negative thinker. So I have some resistance, just as you probably do, to these worst-case scenarios. But I'm convinced that those who try this procedure, which starts out negatively, will ultimately create positive, uplifting, constructive positions of strength. That's what happened to this husband. By imagining *in detail* the worst, he not only was better prepared for disaster, he also began to appreciate more fully the good things that were going on in his marriage.

Worst Case #8:   You lose a child.
I've put this one toward the end, because for many husbands and wives it's the most devastating possibility of all. Losing your spouse would be a terrible thing. But many parents know instinctively that somehow they would pick up the pieces and keep going—especially if there were young children around to be cared for.

But how about the loss of one or more of those children? That's something that our minds often just don't want to accept as a possibility. In one family I know, one of the sons died of cancer before he was ten. Although there were three other children, the father never really recovered. He sank into a state of deep depression and never completely pulled out of it. In fact, the personality change he experienced was so dramatic that his colleagues at work said he had really "become a different person."

As you might expect, the quality of his married life also deteriorated. There was no divorce, but his wife was placed under a terrible burden as he became chronically moody and uncommunicative. There's no happy ending to his story, by the way. This man just accepted his depression as something he would have to live with forever. And his marriage remained in limbo, with a concerned but bewildered wife trying to keep him and their marriage intact from one mood swing to the next.

Is there really any way to prepare for such a devastating event?

Again, I return to what I said about the death of a spouse. The only way you can really prepare for seeing your child pass away before your eyes is to build a strong spiritual commitment throughout your household.

Knowing that your son or daughter has at least tasted a relationship with God is a comfort. But there's more. Great intimacy is required when you bare your soul to your youngster and begin to talk about your own faith. The experience of opening up this way will intensify the quality of that parent-child relationship.

I know one mother and father who provide their son with music lessons, sports activities, private schooling, and other advantages. But in their eyes, the most important thing they give him is an introduction to their faith.

"We started reading children's Bible stories to Thomas when he was only six months old," the mother said. "That's my husband's responsibility, and he and Thomas have stuck with it almost every night for five years now. Also, we make sure Thomas is involved in our church life—he attends Sunday School regularly, and we draw him into any exciting spiritual experiences we have."

The mere thought of losing Thomas is frightening for this couple, too. But if tragedy should befall them, they would have no regrets about the day-by-day quality of their relationship with their son. And most important of all, as they take *present* action to strengthen their own spirituality, they are building a powerful bulwark to handle any threat of personal or family loss.

Worst Case #9:   You get divorced.
We've chosen to eliminate the word *divorce* from our vocabulary for the most part in this book. But now the time has arrived to make an exception. Even I have to admit that there are circumstances where a permanent split must be considered.

Take the case of the spouse who is habitually involved in extramarital affairs. Or the spouse who physically abuses his mate. I recall one case where both of these factors were present.

The husband and wife were both church-goers, but the husband, because of obvious emotional problems, couldn't restrain himself from using his fists on his wife. Also, he periodically got involved in adulterous affairs with other women.

The wife had plenty of legal grounds to end the relationship. But she was convinced that a marrige relationship was a "forever commitment," as she put it. Despite the advice of several counselors, she hung on to even the slightest hope that her husband would change and that their marriage would turn into the ideal Christian union that she visualized in her mind.

But the ideal never became reality. In fact, the situation got worse and it seemed that her health and maybe even her life were in danger.

Finally, she went to a counselor who was able to convince her from Paul's teachings in 1 Corinthians 7 and other passages of Scripture that her husband had in effect destroyed the marriage beyond repair. All that really remained was for her to walk away from something that had ceased to exist.

Not only had he committed adultery—which was a ground for divorce that Jesus recognized—but he also had created a situation where there couldn't be peace in the relationship. And that was a standard that Paul cited as essential in 1 Corinthians 7 if a marriage was to continue.

Finally, she realized that the only answer was to separate

and get a divorce. And she could do so with the knowledge that she had gone above and beyond even the strictest requirements of the New Testament.

But I've purposely avoided suggesting that you picture a divorce in your mind's eye, because I've found that can be counterproductive. For instance, I've noticed that even when couples start *talking* about divorce, even joking about it, that can be a prelude to the real thing.

In any case, I don't want to promote divorce as a viable option. A really tough marriage relationship has got to draw some lines even as far as speculation is concerned. Divorce is too easy a solution. That's a quitter's game, and the objective with a tough marriage relationship is to win—to achieve a strong and viable relationship.

I realize, of course, that sometimes divorce is inevitable. Sometimes, even if you don't want a split, there may be absolutely nothing you can do about it. In fact, in some cases there's nothing you *should* try to do about it. At the same time, however, I firmly believe that most marriages are salvageable—*if* one or preferably both spouses decide to get tough.

It's those pits we've been discussing that threaten a marriage most and tend to raise the specter of divorce most starkly. But even if these traps and tragedies ensnare you for a time, there's always a way that you can escape. And when you do, those mountaintop, peak experiences in your marital relationship seem oh-so-much sweeter.

But whether you find yourself in a pit, on a peak, or somewhere in between, remember this: You're a traveler, not a homesteader. You're on a journey. Your marriage is constantly on the move.

The peaks are like the delightful frosting on a special dessert you savored one evening. They're pleasant and sweet, but not very nourishing—something to appreciate and revel in, not to linger upon. The pits are the ultimate testing sites that will either break a tenuously conditioned marriage or turn it into a love affair of heroic proportions.

Finally, it's the middle ground, the broad expanse of time when nothing really great or terrible is happening, that is the place where you're getting strong and preparing yourself for any contingency.

THE TENTH COMMANDMENT

Master New Tricks

One of the greatest tricks in life is learning to land on your feet. A cat tossed into the air does that with remarkable agility. But in a more figurative sense, when human beings find themselves and their lives upended, they often fall flat on their faces!

Worse yet, when unexpected stresses and strains fling into conflict and confusion, that relationship may actually fall *apart*.

The source of many marital problems is that we lack the ability to respond effectively to new situations and unknown challenges. A little nudge or shove from an unusual direction, and we immediately find ourselves off balance. In short, we react in the same old, predictable ways to new circumstances, and as a result, our marriage relationships suffer and sometimes topple.

But there's a way to avoid this, an approach to married life that involves a series of principles I call the secrets of mastering new tricks.

Secret #1: *Recognize that there's no steady state in your marriage.*

A major failing many spouses have is that they see their marriage as a static relationship. I've heard so many people say, "Oh, if we could just iron out this conflict . . . or achieve that income level . . . or have children who could do this or that, *then* I know we'd truly have a happy marriage."

But such notions betray a faulty assumption that things are supposed to stay the same. Life just isn't like that. As the ancient Greek philosopher Heraclitus said, "There is nothing permanent except change." The basic nature of reality is flux and movement, not stability. So you simply can't take anything for granted too long in your marriage.

Just before he launched his ministry, Jesus was tempted by Satan three times in the wilderness over a forty-day period. During one of those temptations, the devil, knowing that Christ was very hungry, mocked him, daring him to turn some stones into bread. But Jesus said, "It is written, 'Man shall not live by bread alone, but by every word that proceeds from the mouth of God' " (Matthew 4:4). Why did Jesus resist doing what seemed so simple and reasonable?

In effect, Jesus was suggesting here that we shouldn't place our trust only in what we can see and control at any given moment. The temptation for Jesus was to satisfy a momentary need, to make an assumption that a single means of securing food could satisfy and nurture him for the rest of his life. But Jesus knew the devil was offering him a mirage. Life and its demands are not static, and the responses that are required are always changing.

A marriage relationship is a lot like this. There's a temptation to think that one small snippet of life—whether it's a euphoric courtship or some other peak experience—is going to last forever and be the norm for the relationship. But in fact, marriage is always evolving, always changing.

One wife came to me feeling very disturbed because, as she put it, "My husband has gotten so dull! When we were first married, he used to take me on exciting adventures every weekend. But now, he mainly wants to sit around the house."

Further discussions revealed the underlying problem. It seems that her husband was now about fifteen years older. He was working much harder, with far heavier occupational responsibilities than in the first few years of their marriage. Quite frankly, he was worn out when the weekend arrived and just needed time to relax and unwind.

As a matter of fact, he told me that he wanted to recapture a little of the early excitement and adventure of their relationship, too. But he just felt "wrung out and wiped out" on his days off. He needed some time to be rejuvenated before the work week began again.

So, in this marriage as in all others, there was no steady state in the relationship. The spouses—including their individual needs and circumstances—had changed. But this didn't in any way mean that they couldn't rediscover that old excitement. They just had to look for it another way.

What finally worked was that they decided to drive out to a nearby mountain resort about one weekend a month. This spot, which was relatively inexpensive because it was run by a religious group, proved to be just the thing for the new needs and demands of this marriage. The husband could relax; the wife could get her fill of new sights and experiences; and the children had plenty of activities to occupy themselves.

Sure, there may be similarities between a present challenge and one that came months or years before. And you can certainly learn important lessons from past experiences. But in the final analysis, there are going to be at least as many differences as similarities in the new problems you confront as a couple. This means that what's required for success in your marriage is not hard-and-fast formulas but a flexible and fresh attitude to each new wave of change.

Secret #2: Expect new obligations.
In every marriage, financial, moral, and professional obligations are constantly changing, and a truly tough relationship

must be able to absorb these new demands. One of the most difficult set of changes that I have seen in recent years came as a result of the dramatic inflationary trend in the mid- to late 1970s.

Many of the couples I saw during that period were having the most trouble adjusting to changes in their financial capacity as a result of the huge increase in prices. With gas costing more, they had to rethink their vacation and holiday plans. As the price of land soared, they found that they had to reevaluate their assumptions about buying a first home or making a job move to an area, such as California, where real estate prices might be out of reach.

These new financial concerns and obligations put a great deal of pressure on couples who hadn't faced any particular worries about money before. Those who believed that the good economic times of the fifties and sixties would last forever found themselves off balance. In some cases, they even ended up at each other's throats. I still recall one husband who simply couldn't understand why his wife was serving less attractive meals and always seemed to be asking him for more money.

"Why don't you take a look at the budget again?" he asked. "Are you really paying attention to where the money is going?"

She assumed that for some reason he was "out to get her." In fact, until we talked, the real core of the problem never dawned on her—that her husband really didn't realize there was less disposable income around the home to buy the things they had bought before.

When they finally did sit down and go over their income and expenses, they both realized they would have to update their family budget to conform to the new economic circumstances. Now they were able to recognize that a change in their financial obligations had occurred, and this gave them the basis for responding to this change in a constructive way. They were learning new financial tricks.

Secret #3: Control your tendency to panic as you suffer losses.

As a marriage moves forward, many of the changes that occur may also be interpreted as losses suffered by one or both spouses. Often, these losses are associated with age, and the more noticeable they become, the more strain they can put on a relationship. Now, let's look at some of the most important of these losses and see how a fresh approach to them can transform them into gains.

The loss of sexual power. This is a big threat to the confidence and self-image of men especially, and it can turn into a major marital conflict.

At the early stage of a marriage, you develop certain patterns about how you have sex—what you find to be the most exciting techniques, positions, and frequency. But as you grow older, there may be new kinds of stimulation and excitement you need to discover. Eventually, with age, there may also be a change in needs, including how frequently you want to have sex.

For example, we've only recently come to discover in our Western culture some things that Eastern cultures have known for ages: that to achieve a satisfying long-term sexual relationship, it's helpful for the male to learn to withhold ejaculation during intercourse. This allows time for the slower-moving sexual excitement of the female to build.

In the West, young men tend to want to satisfy themselves immediately. They don't have any desire or inclination to exercise control. As a matter of fact, they often measure their sexual prowess by the number of times they can have intercourse in one night.

As a result, in many youthful marriages the wife goes unsatisfied indefinitely. And the husband falls into a pattern that may continue into middle age. A major danger is that as the husband finds his ability to have multiple orgasms slowing down, he begins to get worried because he can't maintain the earlier, youthful pattern by which he measured his sexual attractiveness. He is trapped in a steady-state assumption that the sexual dimension of his marriage shouldn't change.

Unfortunately for many marriages, the husband doesn't realize that *real* sexual skill, where he can consistently satisfy his wife, is probably easier to achieve in middle age than in youth. Why? Because his diminished sex drive can enable him to control and prolong foreplay and intercourse with his wife and thereby give her sexual interest and excitement time to build to mutually satisfying dimensions.

In short, a changing sex drive isn't really a loss at all. Rather, it's an opportunity to learn new "tricks" that can make the bedroom a more exciting place than ever.

Loss of occupational opportunities. For those in their twenties and early thirties, there's often a sense that the possibilities for jobs are almost limitless. In fact, a major frustration during these youthful years comes as young people try to focus their interests and commitment on just one field.

But as a working spouse gets older, he or she usually gets a sense that the possibilities for change and variety in occupations are becoming drastically reduced. Things may be going very well at work. But still, there's a kind of closed-in feeling that the days of easy job change are fast drawing to a close.

This can result in a sense of frustration and even worthlessness, which may cause the affected spouse to look for extramarital affirmation of his worth. Many of the crumbling marriages I encounter are in trouble because a fortyish husband senses his youth is fast disappearing. This belief gets reinforced when he checks around and concludes that he's more or less locked into his current job. So he plunges into an affair with a younger woman in a futile effort to recapture at least a part of his lost youthful identity.

Of course, there's a great deal of truth to the idea that certain opportunities are being shut off by advancing age. Many companies are less interested in hiring a forty-year-old for an entry-level position than they are a twenty-five-year-old. But whether *real* opportunities are shutting down is another issue entirely.

For one thing, very few forty-old-year-olds would be interested in an entry-level position, with the relatively low income and responsibility that would entail. But even more important, some important opportunities may not be closing down at all.

I recall one rather dramatic example, from a highly unlikely quarter, which suggests how increased opportunities can come with age. As a professionally rated pilot myself, I can recall an assumption rampant in military circles some years back that pilots older than thirty-five or so couldn't fly fighters or aerobatic planes. There was especially a great deal of concern that involvement in world-class aerobatic flying—or doing stressful stunts that required many G's of pressure on the body—might be dangerous.

But in fact, older pilots, many in their forties, seemed to do quite well at aerobatics. Many even appeared better able than those in their late teens or early twenties to keep a clear head when the physical strains got toughest. Soon, advances in aeromedicine confirmed the fact that older pilots had developed stiffer arteries, which were able to withstand the pressures and keep their blood circulating better than those who were younger.

The main message here is: don't panic just because you're over forty or fifty! In fact, your advancing years may have prepared you to conquer more new worlds now than ten or twenty years ago. Sometimes you may have to convince others that you're capable. But you'd have to do that if you were younger as well.

The new trick here is learning first not to succumb to the temptation to try to recapture a lost youth that probably wasn't all that great in the first place. Rather, do a serious, in-depth evaluation of exactly what your strengths are right now. Then, look for ways to apply them in the present and future. If you can avoid panic and keep your eyes always looking forward to new possibilities that are present in your changed circumstances, both your inner emotional stability and your marriage will be the major beneficiaries.

Loss of energy. There's no doubt that as we get older, most of us get a little slower. Perhaps you feel a little stiffer when you get out of bed than you did ten years ago. Or you've noticed that you're not quite as quick on the tennis or racketball court.

I sense this physical decline in my own life. I used to be a sprinter when I was in high school, and I also played a number of team sports in college that depended mainly on speed. But I know that today, I'm not as fast as I once was. I may be able to run longer distances today, but that's just because I never tried to run long distances when I was younger.

So, as our energy level, and sometimes even our basic health, declines, we find we just can't do it all anymore. We have to rely on others, including our mates. It's easy to develop a sense of self-sufficiency when you're quite young. You can work and play for long hours and get by on very little sleep. But as you get older, you need to pace yourself more and perhaps set aside additional rest periods.

One forty-five-year-old husband I know got very cranky when he tried to escalate his physical activity but then discovered his body wasn't up to it. He started training for a marathon and at the same time was playing on the squash ladder in his local club. Things went just fine for a month or so. But then he began to feel quite fatigued. He needed more and more sleep and couldn't focus his attention as well on his work. His constant tiredness also made him become much testier with his wife and children.

Then his body simply rebelled. On the squash court one day, he lost control of his legs at the end of the final game of a particularly tough match. He crashed into the wall and severely sprained his ankle.

The torn ligaments required that a cast be placed on his leg, and he had to get around on crutches for about a month. If he had been younger, the injury would undoubtedly have been less severe and the healing process would also have been quicker. But there he was, an invalid for a month. And for the first time in memory, he had to rely on his wife to do all sorts of things around the house that had been his joy and responsibility. She even had to drive him to work each morning.

This man didn't take well at first to this change in his circumstances. But then, gradually, he learned some new tricks. For one thing, he realized he would simply have to sit back and allow his wife to care for him because he could no longer maintain even an illusion of self-sufficiency. Also, he had to slow his life down and cut out many of the extraneous activities in which he had become involved. There was more time now for him to lie around and talk to other family members, especially his wife.

Once he got over the initial frustration of feeling like an invalid, this husband actually came to value the new role that a sprained ankle thrust upon him. And when he finally put aside the crutches, he continued to observe the lessons he had learned. For one thing, he avoided getting overinvolved in outside sports and other time-consuming activities. But most important of all, he became more aware of the importance of being able to depend on others.

Loss of children. The loss I'm talking about here is not really physical death, though certainly death could be included. Rather, I'm referring to the "empty nest," when the children grow up and move away to college and the working world.

This involves a big change in the relationship of husband and wife because they are thrust together as never before. It's easy to panic at this point. One spouse may worry, Will we ever be able to pick up our old relationship and regain the intimacy lost while the kids were our focus? The other may think, We've simply grown apart. Now, without the children to keep us together, we might as well get a divorce because that's where we are anyway!

As far as I'm concerned, neither of these approaches is acceptable. There are plenty of things you can do to fill that empty nest instead of becoming remorseful or depressed about the children leaving.

Actually, I prefer to think of the "open nest" rather than the "empty nest." For example, if you really like having kids around so much, you might take in some student boarders. Or you could regard the departure of the children as a fabulous opportunity to have an entirely new set of adventures as a married couple—such as traveling to far-flung locales or getting involved more deeply in service work for the needy.

To begin to learn these new tricks, however, it's necessary first of all to push any negative thoughts about your marital relationship out of your mind. Then, focus on the range of available possibilities, and you'll find that all sorts of exciting prospects come to mind.

Loss of upward economic mobility. After you reach a certain age, it's almost inevitable that you'll notice that a kind of ceiling has appeared over your career and economic aspirations. For example, you might work hard to get a big deal completed, one you're certain will pave the way to the next promotion. But the promotion doesn't come because a younger person is given the position. This disappointment may trigger a realization that you probably won't be earning any more money or furthering your social or career status. You're at the top of your personal career ladder and there's nowhere to go but down.

Another way of describing this disturbing dilemma is that you realize that your one great dream will never materialize. Your youthful fantasies from the early years of marriage about "what I want to become during my life" will never become quite the reality that was promised.

I still recall in my sixth-grade class that the teacher asked all the children in the room to say what they wanted to be when they grew up. There were four guys in that small rural township schoolroom who seemed to me unlikely to reach the top of any field. Yet they all said, confidently, "I want to be president of the United States."

I've thought of their response many times since then, and I've wondered what happened to them when their dreams never even came close to being realized. At the same time, I've understood that, for all of us, our dreams always run ahead of reality. And they should! That's part of what dreams are for—to stretch our minds and stimulate our imaginations. But at the end, there's always some remorse because we haven't lived up to our full potential.

I remember with a heavy heart the speech that General Douglas MacArthur made after President Truman pulled him back from Korea. General MacArthur was a man I very much admired. In fact, as a kid growing up, I idealized him because he had been so successful, leading all those military campaigns and rising to the rank of five-star general.

At the time, it was impossible for me to conceive that he hadn't fulfilled all his dreams. Yet he said in his final speech before the U.S. Congress that there were many things he had wanted to do in his life that had never come to pass. It was important for me to hear these words from a person I held in such high esteem; he helped to put my own life and aspirations in perspective. In subsequent years, I have sometimes thought of General MacArthur when trying to understand the dreams and needs of those I counsel.

Few of us ever achieve all we want to achieve. We probably will never reach an ultimately satisfying plateau in our lives. But unless we realize that the gold ring of earthly achievement will most likely always remain just out of our grasp, we're setting ourselves up to be frustrated. Moreover, the frustration from unfulfilled childhood dreams may taint our relationship with our spouses. The marriage itself may become the object of scorn and pain, simply because we can't grow up.

There are many new tricks a person may devise to meet such a challenge. One may refuse to accept the fact that there is, indeed, a ceiling on one's career opportunities. In such a case, either husband or wife might turn into a workaholic, determined to *force* a way to greater heights of achievement, or be willing to die in the attempt.

More likely, though, the immature spouse, unwilling to learn new tricks, will eventually just give up, get frustrated or depressed, and then take the dissatisfaction out on the marital partner. It has nothing to do with the spouse, of course, but he or she becomes the target. And unless the partner is a very strong, compassionate person, their marriage may begin to head for the rocks.

But I've found that there's another solution that works much better. That's a way that has been opened up for us by God. If our dreams are centered on Him, and not on career, social status, or money, then we're more likely to take the "slings and arrows of outrageous fortune" with greater equanimity.

With a divine viewpoint in mind, a person shouldn't have any less ambition or drive to achieve and excel. But he should possess a keener sense of perspective about how his career or other goals fit into the big picture of life, including the all-important relationship with family and spouse. Indeed, a firm religious faith is the greatest "trick" of all in dealing with the panic-producing situations in our lives.

Loss of friends or loved ones. This is one of those life changes that is inevitable, but that fact doesn't make the event any less wrenching. The loss could come through death, through a falling out because of a personality disagreement, or even through a move to another part of the country.

In such a case, any sense of steady state in our lives is suddenly lost. A marriage may seem to remain strong during turbulence in other relationships. But the added pressures have to cause one or both spouses to become preoccupied for a time with the loss they've experienced outside the marriage.

During these times, the burden of support will be on the spouse who has suffered less from the loss of the friend or loved one. I recall one case where a couple moved into our area after the husband had been given a lucrative promotion with his company. Everything in their lives seemed on the up-swing—money, career, social position. But still, the wife was miserable. Why? Because she had been forced to leave all her friends and family network back in the community they had left.

She sank into periodic depressions and had great difficulty meeting new people. Somehow she just couldn't get moti-vated to be aggressive in making new friends. As a result, she spent much of the day moping around the house. Also, it didn't help that their home, a beautiful, rambling place set on several wooded acres, was so isolated that there were no neighbors within easy walking distance.

For a while, this couple couldn't even figure out what the problem was. After a couple of counseling sessions, however, it became apparent that all she needed was to get outside herself and begin to make some friends. In this case, it was the husband who had to take the initiative, since his wife had become almost immobilized by her lapses into depression.

So he set aside several hours and made some phone calls to various service organizations and churches that he felt might meet his wife's needs. And that's what finally did the trick.

It's true that the wife did resist taking the first steps to meet the people her husband had called; the husband ac-tually had to go around with her to bolster her courage. But after the initial contact, she quickly found some organizations that she fit into. And soon she was as involved with outside interests and friends in her new neighborhood as she had been in her old.

In this case, the wife's main weakness was that she was a passive person who simply had trouble getting started. She was a little insecure and timid about meeting new people. So her husband, who was much more aggressive, filled in this de-ficiency in her personality.

His act of reaching out to help his wife was an important technique, if you want to call it that, in enabling her—and by inference, their marriage—to get over the trauma of change connected with a physical move. In addition, his gesture and her acceptance of his loving action were clear signs that the two spouses were truly on the way to becoming one in their marriage. This husband truly saw himself and his wife as a unified entity in which his strengths could overcome his wife's weaknesses and vice versa. And that's exactly what happened in this situation.

Secret #4:   Learn to be intimate.
Being physically close together, whether in a bed, on a living room sofa, in a theater, or in a car driving along the highway, is not the same as intimacy. Being intimate begins when each partner in the marriage willingly gives some personal "prime time" to the other and to the relationship.

Instead of "debriefing" your spouse in a perfunctory way at the end of a busy, exhausting day, you might introduce some intimacy over a lingering cup of morning coffee. Or you might occasionally meet after work at a small, out of the way pastry shop, apart from the maddening crowd of children and the disrupting jangle of telephones.

Sometimes, you might also want to have a quiet, uninterrupted lunch together. Or your tête-à-tête may take place in those private, special moments when you serve each other a favorite brew of hot tea in the late evening before you retire.

Praying together as a couple can also become a creative ritual for developing intimacy. Sharing the spiritual times together, a couple can reveal themselves to one another and to God. This mutual self-revelation in a prayer-and-share time promotes not a vulnerable dependency but rather individual and mutual strength—and a genuine toughness in the marriage.

Dealing with the "pits" in the marriage through intimacy allows the couple the opportunity to know one another completely. And that means experiencing the most intimate social, spiritual, sexual, and conversational moments.

Intimacy undoubtedly provides the best base for effective

communication. Neither partner in the marriage has to sec-
ond-guess what the other is thinking. So intimacy allows
either spouse to say with honesty and deep candor, "I'm
really feeling down today, and I want you to know that if I
seem withdrawn or snappy it's not because of you; it's because of what's going on with me." This invites the other to
accept and receive an honest exposure of feelings without
moralizing, or responding with an emotional sledge-hammer,
or simply withdrawing.

Similarly, when one of the marriage partners has a particular concern about the family, the home, or work, that partner
should feel confident enough to suggest in the intimate setting of personal conversation, "Here's my thought about our
vacation." Or, "Here is an idea I think will work at the office.
I want to know what you think about it. Should we try this?"
Such intimacy goes beyond physical and sexual intimacy to
daily and sometimes mundane moral, spiritual, and work relations.

Finally, a sign of true intimacy is that one feels present
and in a sense *is* present with the other marriage partner,
even when physical separation intervenes. One of the first
miracles that Jesus did was to heal the Roman centurion's
servant *at a distance*. The centurion showed he experienced both authority and intimacy when he made it clear
to Jesus that he knew Christ didn't have to come physically
to his home to heal his servant. Jesus said that such faith
was not at all in evidence in his own hometown, where
people should by definition be trustful and intimate. Intimacy can even fill physical distances with a transcendent
closeness.

Now, let me say just one word about making mistakes as
you learn the art of mastering new tricks in your marriage. In
my work as a part-time flight instructor, I've noticed something important about the life-saving function of the *process*
of learning from your mistakes.

Almost universally, a student pilot will have a particular kind of trouble during landing. I'm not talking about bumping or skidding the plane as it hits the runway. Rather, there's a tendency for most people to drift off to the left of the runway. Called the "center line drift on final approach," this error occurs because of a peculiar rudder movement that must be made to keep the plane properly aligned with the runway.

Although I sometimes tell my students that flying is somewhat like driving a car, the analogy breaks down with this movement. In this case, you simply can't transfer what you've learned in an automobile; you have to make your mistakes and learn this particular skill in the air.

But I had one student who landed flawlessly from the very beginning; he never made this particular mistake of drifting off to the left. At first, I was amazed. The longer I watched him, however, the more concerned I got, and my worry deepened as the time drew near for him to solo.

Specifically, I was frightened because I didn't want him to go up in that plane alone without making this particular mistake and knowing how to correct it. The process of going through the mistake and then having the experience of correcting it is usually considered essential for a person to become adept at a safe landing.

"You know, you're the first student I've ever had who hasn't had trouble with what we call the center line drift on the final approach," I finally told him. Then I explained what the mistake was and added, "I don't know whether you really know how to do this or whether you've been lucky."

"Well, I'm not sure," he replied, "but would it help you to know that when I was a teenager I drove combines during the summer? They had rear-wheel steering and brake pedals that have the same kind of action as the rudder pedals on the airplane."

That explained it, and I gave a sigh of relief. Because this fellow had spent hours and hours going through this unusual rudder maneuver on a land-based vehicle, I didn't have to worry about him in the air. He had mastered this particular trick in an unexpected and highly unorthodox way. But still, he had mastered it—and that was what counted.

Whether in the air or in a marriage relationship, we'll always encounter surprises and unsettling conditions that may threaten to throw us off our stride. At the same time, I've discovered that there's always a way of escaping from the traps that accompany change. It's just a matter first of finding an effective approach, technique, insight, or even trick that suits the situation.

This solution may be a psychological ploy or it may be rooted in a deeply spiritual understanding of life. But in the last analysis, it must also be practical. The best response to the change and turmoil that challenge our marriages consistently demands that we have the courage to act.

The proverbial cat lands on its feet because it responds *actively* to an inner sense of equilibrium and balance. It's much the same with us. We must be attuned to those still, small voices within, and at the same time be willing to move forward when we finally hear that which we know, down deep, to be correct.

THE ELEVENTH COMMANDMENT

Fight for Some Solitude

I've said a great deal in this book about the importance of the two partners becoming one in a marriage. I've also stressed the importance of serving your mate, subordinating your interests, and giving a priority to the relationship rather than the individual.

But there is a point at which the giving and emptying of yourself in favor of your spouse has to stop and personal nurturance must begin. Otherwise, you'll be in danger of becoming an empty shell with nothing left to share.

One way of looking at this situation is that you and your spouse are individuals with separate spiritual springs that need filling. And the best way to find those sources of inner succor is to retreat from the hullabaloo of life to a place of personal solitude and silence. There, you can reflect on where you're going and where you've been. And you can begin to replenish those inner reservoirs of peace that tend to evaporate in the face of life's daily pressures.

Solitude is a necessity, not a luxury. But you're probably going to have to fight for it! And the fight will have to be waged on several fronts.

- First, there's the *time-pressure front*. With an overpacked schedule and mounting demands from other people, including your family, you may think you just can't take any time off to "feed" yourself spiritually.
- Then, there's the *guilt front*. Even if you can find some free time, you are reluctant to take it and use it for yourself because you sense that maybe the time could be used more productively in some other way. Isn't it better, for example, to spend an extra hour or two on your family or work than on personal prayer and reflection?
- Finally, there's the *family-pressure front*. This ties in directly with guilt considerations. Typically, when you say you're going to take some time to be alone, your spouse may think or *say*, "You're selfish; you're abandoning me; you're neglecting the children."

You shouldn't take such a response negatively. Your spouse is just indicating he needs you. But at the same time, you can't allow yourself to be swayed. You have to monitor your inner being and guard your periods of solitude wisely. The chances are, as the positive results of your time of private meditation and reflection help strengthen your relationships, your spouse will see the benefits. Then he'll stop complaining or sulking.

Your goal in seeking solitude, by the way, shouldn't be to reach some peak of spiritual perfection overnight. Instead, it's important to try for the middle ground. This means making a personal commitment of time that will be within the realm of possibility, given your busy schedule. I would suggest that you begin by setting aside ten minutes a day and working to an hour a day to get the maximum benefits. In any case, there's nothing wrong with going for a shorter period of time at the outset.

But how exactly can you make the best use of a time of personal reflection?

To answer this question, and to get you started on the road to productive times of solitude, let me suggest five principles of individual prayer and meditation that have enhanced the relationship of many husbands and wives.

1. You have to be alone.

It all starts with this principle. If you've chosen a physical location where you're constantly being interrupted, you've lost the fight for solitude before you even get started. The main point is to be free from outside intrusions and demands. So your time of retreat has to be physical as well as mental.

Sometimes, just locking the bedroom door isn't enough. If you find there simply isn't a place in your home, you might try a solution that I personally have used on many occasions—just take a walk! There's something about the fresh air and freedom to stroll at your own pace that begins to revive your spirit, even without any focused meditation or prayer.

One college student I knew a few years ago had the habit of walking long distances each day, even in the dead of winter. It might have been bitter cold, but she would still dress up like an Eskimo and head outside.

It wasn't just the scenery, she explained, nor was it the quality of the air, though both of these factors were a welcome change from her room. Rather, it was the best way for her to get off alone with her thoughts and dreams. No matter how tired or rotten she felt, the walk always picked her up again.

But whatever place you choose, it has to provide a sense of complete solitude.

2. Pick some thought, issue, or passage of Scripture for contemplation.

The purpose at this point is just to discipline your mind to focus for a time on some topic. If you let your mind wander all over the place during your time of solitude, that's better than nothing. But the greatest benefits come as you begin to do some quiet thinking and reflection.

For example, you might start out by directing your thinking for half the time of your walk along the following lines:

- *Contemplate yourself as a part of the greater scheme of reality.* This might involve a focus on birth, death, changing seasons, animals, or the plant life around you. Everyone and everything has its place in the overall plan—and that includes you.

  We're all connected in some way to each other. As your mind ranges off your immediate problems to some of the broader movements and questions in the universe, you'll find yourself settling down inside. You'll become more philosophical about your own pressures and gain a better perspective on things. You'll probably even find that anxieties and worries you are harboring begin to lessen. Peace will come easier, even at this very early stage of your experience of solitude.

- *Contemplate your emotional and physical well-being.* I always find it helpful to identify exactly how I'm feeling and, if possible, why I'm feeling that way. If you're feeling harried or pressured, ask yourself what forces are causing these feelings. Also, check out your physical state: Ask, Is my diet really sufficient? Do I get enough rest? How much sleep did I get last night? Is my body trying to tell me something, through feelings of discomfort or pain?

- *Contemplate your relationships.* Focus on each of your family, loved ones, and business colleagues. How do you get along with them? Do you let them know you care about them? Are you spending enough time on the relationships you value the most? It's somewhat ironic that the periods of time we spend away from our loved ones in nurturing solitude can actually help to bring us closer together.

- *Contemplate the future.* This is potentially a dangerous one because contemplating the future can easily turn into *living* in the future. But the idea here is to keep your thoughts under a degree of control. You don't want to plan the future at this point, just muse a little about it.

You might ask, Where am I headed in my life? What are my ultimate goals? Am I on the track or heading off on a tangent?

3. Spend time alone with the Bible every day.

This third principle of effective solitude is one of the most important in keeping your thoughts on a productive track. Here, I'm not talking about Bible study. Rather, what you should concentrtate on is reading a passage of Scripture in a listening mode. In this way, you'll allow God to talk to you rather than impose your own or somebody else's preconceptions on the Bible. Many who use this approach have found that fifteen to thirty minutes is an optimum time frame for such devotional reading. But you may need to begin with just five to ten minutes to get into "spiritual shape."

The Scriptures have tremendous power to redirect our thinking and fill us with inspiration. Practically every powerful personality in the Judeo-Christian tradition—from King David to St. Paul to Martin Luther to John Wesley—has drawn spiritual sustenance from regular daily exposure to the Scriptures.

So first, you should choose a quiet place; then, you should begin to practice focused thinking and contemplation, and thirdly, you should add further spiritual content and direction to your time alone by listening to God in the Scriptures.

By this point, after you're about thirty or forty minutes into your time of solitude, the cares of the day should have faded into the background. Your mind is more settled; also, you have a broader, healthier perspective on the cares and concerns of your life. Now the time has arrived to move your solitary time into an action mode so that you're ready to start doing something about those problems.

4. Spend part of your time of solitude in prayer.
I advise placing the actual prayer time in the last part of a period of contemplation because it's too easy to start out with some quick requests for God. Then the tendency may be to "close up the prayer shop" and be on our way after just a few minutes.

In contrast, when you've cleared your mind of distractions with more general contemplation and Bible reading, you're likely to have much more patience and a better sense of perspective as you begin to talk to God directly.

Also, even when active conversation with God begins, I think it's a good idea not to focus immediately on requests or supplications. There are other types of prayers that are just as important as asking for things. As a result, I recommend the prayer sequence reflected in the tried-and-true prayer formula of the acronym ACTS:

A—adoration, such as praising God and telling him you love him;

C—confession of your mistakes and wrongdoings, including those involving your marriage;

T—thanksgiving for all the blessings God has given you, your spouse, and your family;

S—supplication for your needs and those of your spouse, your family, and other people who concern you.

Sometimes, of course, we have something so pressing on our minds that we just have to get it out on the table before God right at the beginning—maybe even before those initial periods of contemplation and Scripture reading.

For example, when I've counseled couples who were having problems with their marriage, I've sometimes found that an entire period of private contemplation was best devoted to asking God a specific question. This might be, What can be done to introduce love back into my marriage? Or, What can I do to help my wife experience more joy in her life?

Whatever the question, it may be so pressing that it has to be asked of God over and over, in a series of your private times of contemplation. And you may have to sit quietly listening for God's answer without filling the silence with any words or readings of your own.

Jesus, you know, spent all night in prayer before he chose the twelve apostles (see Luke 6). And I suspect that much of his prayer time was spent asking the question Whom shall I pick? and then waiting for a response from the Father.

But most times, I think it's best to leave the requests off until the very end. Then, we're more inclined to listen for God's will rather than try to impose our own wills on Him.

How much time should be devoted to this period of active prayer? I think fifteen minutes is a minimum; and often you may find yourself going for far longer periods of times.

5. Spend time in creating a vision for your life.
During the initial time of contemplation, right at the beginning of your time of solitude, you may have reflected briefly on your goals in life. But it's also a good idea to set aside a lengthier period of time for this purpose.

Where do you want to be in one year? Five years? Ten years? Are your present activities moving you toward these objectives?

And it's important to remember that this time of creating your own personal vision of life can't be limited to material things. In fact, as you think about the things that really matter in your life, you'll probably find that the money, status, and even career don't matter that much.

Relationships *are* important, however—especially your relationship with your spouse and children. Also, it's essential to consider the way in which you're moving or *not* moving toward those family, marital, and spiritual goals that you consider important.

Sometimes, the sense of overall direction and vision may come in a flash as you're reading the Bible. Or it may come as you're contemplating your life in the general flow of other lives. But however the insight arrives, it's important to set aside some time for reflection about "where I am going and where I want to be at some point in the future." It's only by raising these questions, contemplating them, and praying about them that you can exercise some control in making your visions a reality.

Finally, solitude is a time to be alone but *never* a time for escape. It's not a time simply to get away from the family. And if you are interrupted, the appropriate response is not, "You're ruining my time alone with God!"

Actually, Jesus was interrupted numerous times while he was praying or about to begin praying. His response? He always gave precedence to human need and contact. Of course, he did fight for his solitude by doing everything he could to find a quiet time with the Father—even if it meant heading up into the hills before dawn or spending all night in prayer while everyone else was getting some shut-eye. If he was interrupted, he immediately embraced the people who were approaching him; and then he came back later to his solitary relationship with the Father.

But in the end he always sought out solitude, even after interruptions. He knew that it was essential to be filled up spiritually even as he was emptying himself in the service of others.

A marriage is much like this. In a strong, tough relationship, each spouse must be ready constantly to serve the other. But at the same time, some solitude is necessary for each individual as a means to replenish those depleted spiritual, emotional, and physical resources. Then, when you've been filled up with God's power, you're ready to return to the exciting interplay of the relationship.

So always be ready to fight for your solitude. It's a sine qua non for joyful togetherness.

THE TWELFTH COMMANDMENT

Learn to Let Go

We've explored in detail various ways of holding on to your relationship with your spouse. Now, with this final commandment, the time has arrived to let go.

What exactly does it mean to let go?

Probably the best way of describing this concept comes from E. Stanley Jones, who in his classic book *Christian Maturity* puts it like this: "Let go and let God." The essence of this principle is that even as we get actively involved in life— including marriage—we have to recognize there are limits beyond which we can't have a decisive influence on the future course of events. We *may* be able to exercise some control up to a certain point. But beyond that point, the influence of other factors and other people becomes decisive.

Still, there is hope for those regions of our lives that lie well beyond our own powers. Even as our influence fades away, God's influence can grow stronger—*if* we allow Him to help us. And with our relinquishing of control comes a deep sense of peace and security, rooted in the knowledge that omnipotent forces are now in charge.

As far as your marriage is concerned, there are some special areas where a release of control to God is most likely to be effective. It's true, of course, that with the biblical approach *all* of our lives, including the entire marital relationship, should be placed under God's control. But still, it's helpful to pinpoint a few key places where it's essential to concentrate on letting go.

Let Go of False Assumptions About Marriage

Our society has drawn together two misconceptions into a "package deal" that many of us have tried to incorporate into our marriages.

One of these misconceptions is a false model of marriage that we've picked up from both the print and electronic media. For example, the Sunday comics have made Dagwood and Blondie a permanent part of our matrimonial ethos. They are the lovable couple who have certain problems, but none are that important. And all are always resolved in some pleasant way by the end of the strip. This image has been carried on by television, with Ozzie and Harriet, Archie and Edith, Bob and Joanna of *Newhart*, and many others.

The other misconception comes from our commercials and consumer habits. We've come to believe that either there is a quick-fix solution to our problems or we can just throw away the used-up can, bottle, wrapper—or relationship. Unfortunately, marriage sometimes gets defined in terms of these two misconceptions. In other words, it's supposed to be all fun, humorous and relatively easy. And if for some reason the relationship doesn't work in these terms—and work *fast*—we can just get rid of it.

An important first step, then, is to begin to identify these and other false assumptions about life in general and marriage in particular. Next, it's necessary to consciously let go of

them. In their place, we must substitute assumptions that say
marriage is meant to be permanent.

Let Go of Your Old Definitions of Adulthood

When we try to imagine ourselves in the full flower of adulthood, most of us come up with an idealized image—one in
which we're at the absolute height of our human powers. We
see ourselves as physically and mentally adept, sexually attractive, and at the peak of our personal and professional
skills.

But in this fantasy-based image of ourselves, we forget
some very important factors. We forget the whole process of
aging, for example. Ironically, even as we reach the height of
experience and skill, we begin to decline in physical energy
and strength. Also, our physical beauty begins to fade, and
with it goes at least some degree of sexual attractiveness.

But we're often not willing to accept these changes. We
don't want to let go of our ingrained ideas of what it means to
be a complete adult and then receive new assumptions that
conform more truly to reality.

So you may have a fifty-five-year-old man who is at the
height of his career but by no means at the height of his physical power and attractiveness. Yet he may still try to recapture
in some way that bodily dimension of his lost youth by chas-
ing and marrying a nineteen-year-old girl.

The same false sense of ideal adulthood may ensnare this
older man's female counterpart. I know one widow in her late
fifties who suddenly decided to shorten and tighten her skirts,
dye her hair, and make herself available for one-night stands
with much younger men.

She was fairly attractive for her age, and her ready availabil-
ity and willingness to foot the entertainment bills did gain her
some liaisons with younger men. But ultimately, she began to
feel used, and her attempt to become a frivolous belle of the
ball again just didn't succeed.

This sort of regression is especially sad to me because these mature people have so much to give to others, including those much younger. But instead, they focus exclusively on a false image they have constructed of themselves—an image they won't release because they think it reflects what the perfect attractive and effective adult should be like.

What kind of image of adulthood would be more appropriate for those of us who have reached middle age and are heading into the years beyond?

There are two important qualities I'd like to see incorporated into the mature adult personality: a childlike attitude, and a burning desire to become a sage. I believe that a proper understanding and acceptance of these goals can help us to become both better individuals and better mates. So now, let me explain both of these attributes in a little more detail.

1. The childlike attitude. Jesus said that to know God—to be spiritually and emotionally mature—we must "become as little children" (Matthew 18:3). But how can this be? Is there any way to explain the paradox that to become effective adults we must in some way revert to childhood? To cast some light on this saying of Christ, we have to consider in some depth what the most attractive qualities of a child are.

- To begin with, a little child is *totally dependent* on his parents or guardians. He is completely trusting. He believes anything his parents tell him and begins to fall into a rhythm of imitating the parent.

   In a similar vein, in any successful marriage relationship we must first recognize our dependence on God. That means trusting Him in those situations we can't control and listening to Him and following without question as He guides us through hard times and difficult challenges.
- A little child is also *persistent, tireless, and energetic* in work and play. Probably as part of the innate learning process, little kids will keep at repetitive, boring tasks almost indefinitely.

One two-year-old boy I know insisted on having his own toy vacuum cleaner so that he could follow his father around as he cleaned up the garage. And he wanted to keep going long after Dad had stopped.

That same tireless persistence, aimed at resolving seemingly minor conflicts, is what can help get a marriage over the rough spots and bad times. If you see some area where you and your spouse tend to get involved in fights or just can't seem to work together, don't give up! Take the long view—your marriage is a life-long commitment. Then work steadily, lovingly, and diligently to make your marriage a more harmonious whole.

- A child has a *sense of wonder.* The ability to see the new, the exciting, and the humorous in the small, ordinary things of life is one of the greatest capacities of small children. Every new experience with them is fun and refreshing.

One colleague of mine found his outlook on life was transformed by his first child, who saw a side of life that the father, with his "adult" image of himself, had missed. The little boy saw special meaning in little specks on the wall, configurations in paintings, and the first crocuses of spring. He could spot a single bird far up in a tree and become fascinated contemplating it—a skill his father had abandoned far back in childhood.

Adults tend to ignore such things when they're in the midst of their hectic daily schedules. But when they're around children, their capacity for experiencing joy in small things is greatly increased. And that's the joy that happened to my colleague.

- Children are uninhibited in showing *affection.* It's hard to find an infant or toddler who doesn't like to be kissed or hugged. You and your spouse have the same need, and most likely you expressed yourself in these romantic ways during courtship.

In recent years, however, you may have neglected practicing some of the affectionate gestures, like a squeeze, a kiss, or even a smile. But that doesn't mean the need to give and receive open affection has disappeared. You and your mate require plenty of affection, and a child can show you something about how to express it.

- Children are wonderful *imitators.* When the child of a friend of mine saw his father typing a letter on the family typewriter, the youngster immediately jumped into his father's lap. And he wouldn't get down until he was allowed to do some typing himself.

Of course, children imitate the bad as well as the good. If you let a "shut up" or other epithet slip out in front of a pre-schooler, you'll almost certainly hear the same word coming right back at you in short order.

In our marriages, we also should imitate the good things we see in happy, strong relationships. St. Paul said in his first let-ter to the church at Corinth, "Be imitators of me, as I am of Christ" (1 Corinthians 11:1). In our marriages, as in every other dimension of our lives, we must be very careful to choose the very best models to follow. Otherwise, we may find ourselves emulating relationships and values that can only lead to failure and unhappiness.

- Little children need to spend a *sufficient amount of time with their parents.* More and more is being written these days about the importance of parents putting in plenty of time with their kids. The so-called quality time is important, but so is *quantity* of time. Parents can't spend only a few minutes with their children each day and then expect surrogates, nannies, teachers, and baby-sitters to take up all the slack.

It's the same way with our marriages. Husbands and wives need to spend a considerable amount of time together, and they also need to spend regular amounts of time in the com-pany of their Perfect Parent, God. It's only as spouses relate to one another in God's presence that they can hope to find the most fruitful directions for their relationship.

2. The desire to become a sage. This second important quality of mature adulthood can best be summed up in the word *sage.* A sage is a person who is characterized by great wisdom, a wisdom that often comes from vast experi-ence and advancing years.

The sage differs from many other aging adults in that he often has had a vision years before of what he wanted to be-come. I know one thirty-year-old, for example, who has started asking himself, "What will satisfy me most when I reach age sixty-five and look back on my life?"

For this young man, the answer is not wealth, social status, or career success, though he would like to have those things. Rather, the most satisfying thing to him would be his relationships with other human beings, including his wife and children.

He wants to be able to look back and say in his later years that he was able to help others and contribute to their growth as well as his own. In short, he knows that the quality of his human relationships will be the key to later happiness. So he has begun *today* to strengthen those relationships for the future. This young man in effect has a vision of himself as a sage. And he will become one if he keeps on this track.

In the context of the marital bond, sagedom takes on a special meaning. For example, one couple I know who are now in their mid-forties have gone through a series of spiritual developments in recent years. When they first got married, the wife was a committed Christian, and the husband was an agnostic. In other words, they were quite far apart in their basic spiritual assumptions, and this difference gave rise to some conflicts in the way they related to each other, to friends, and to their children.

After they had been married for about five years, the husband underwent a conversion experience. But even then, they didn't immediately get on the same spiritual wavelength. The wife sometimes acted in a condescending way to her husband's lack of spiritual experience. That made him angry, and he would periodically decide he was going to "throw this religious thing over" and revert to his old agnosticism.

But somehow he managed to stick with the faith. And gradually his wife became more sensitive to his needs. One of the most important things she learned was just to keep out of his way while he was going through some of the early stages of spiritual growth.

Finally, when they both reached their forties, they found

that they were more or less on a par in spiritual terms. And for the first time, they began to work together toward certain spiritual goals: They started moving in tandem to rear their children in a way consistent with their values; they labored side by side in building up a religious-education program at their church; and soon younger couples began to seek them out for advice.

In short, this couple has now just reached the stage where they are becoming "married sages" who are in a position to provide spiritual advice to other couples in need. It's really a beautiful thing to watch as they share with others the mistakes they've made and lessons they've learned. Most important of all, they are living examples of how two married people can let go of certain notions about themselves and their marriage. And having "let go and let God," they are beginning to affirm together an entirely new concept of a spiritually based relationship.

In the last analysis, this final commandment sums up all the rest. When we learn to let go of our lives—to lose ourselves in the needs of others and in those truths that far transcend our own limited existence—that's when we are finally ready to build a tough and viable relationship.

The greatest source of worry, anxiety, and unhappiness is the feeling that the burdens of your life rest entirely on your own shoulders. It's impossible for any one person to resolve all the complex problems of his individual life, his marriage and family life, and his dealings with friends and acquaintances outside the family. So it's comforting to know that we can release our problems to a concerned and compassionate spouse and to a loving and all-powerful God.

Finally, the act of letting go transcends mere problems and issues. It also encompasses the release of people—including your spouse—from your control. You may be confronting an especially intractable problem in relating to your husband or wife. You've tried every trick and technique you can think of to break through the walls that have been erected between the two of you. You've attempted every form of control, influence, and manipulation you know, but all to no avail. This is a classic case where it can work wonders to let go and consciously put that spouse in the hands of God.

Learning to let go is usually not an overnight process, however. It can take a lifetime. So the sooner you get started, the more freedom and power you'll feel in encouraging the growth and development of your marital relationship. A tough marriage, after all, is one that can carry you and your mate through every wrenching and divisive challenge that life can offer. Yet a genuinely tough relationship will still leave you in a position where you love each other more deeply than ever. And you'll know beyond any doubt that you have somehow merged into one.